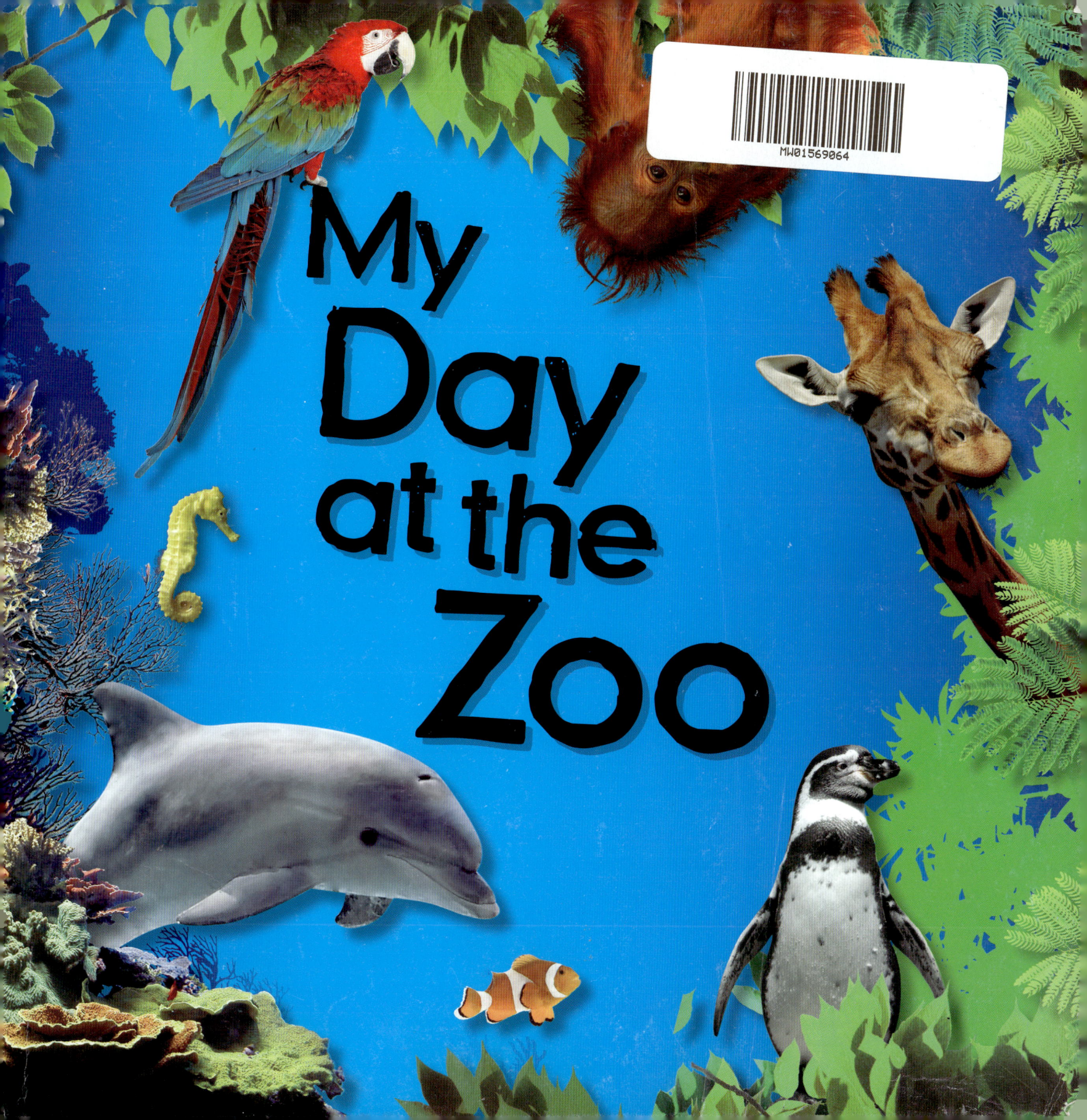
My Day at the Zoo

Consultant: Steve Parker
Editor: Eve Marleau
Designer and
Picture Researcher: Liz Wiffen

Copyright © QEB Publishing 2010
Published in the United States by
QEB Publishing, Inc
3 Wrigley, Suite A
Irvine, CA 92618

www.qed-publishing.co.uk

All rights reserved. No part of this publication may be reproduced, stored in a retrieval system, or transmitted in any form or by any means, electronic, mechanical, photocopying, recording, or otherwise, without the prior permission of the publisher, nor be otherwise circulated in any form of binding or cover other than that in which it is published and without a similar condition being imposed on the subsequent purchaser.

A CIP record for this title is available from the Library of Congress.

ISBN 978 1 60992 059 3

Printed in China

Picture credits: t=top, b=bottom, r=right, l=left, c=centre
Alamy 95 WILDLIFE GmbH
Getty 65b Leticia Lovo
Nature Picture Library: 104bl Doug Perrine, 106 tr Kim Taylor, 107 tl Mark Bowler, 107 tl Jurgen Freud, 107 bl Nature Production, 108 bl Brandon Cole, 109 tr Sue Daly.
NHPA 95b Norbert Wu, 103t Kevin Schafer
Photolibrary: 5t Zoological Society / San Diego, 8t Vivek Sinha, 20r John Cancalosi, 21t Nigel Pavitt, 35t, 39c, 41t, 45, 47c, 49t, 49c, 54, 60b JTB Photo, 61t JTB Photo, 61b Wayne Lynch, 68b jspix jspix, 73b Mark Jones, 75b Mike Powles, 86c Javier Larrea, 88b Poelzer Poelzer, 89t Norbert Probst, 89b Reinhard Dirscherl, 90b Paul Kay, 91c Tobias Bernhard, 96t David B Fleetham, 98c Paul Kay, 101t Peter Walton, 103b Alberto Muro Pellicon.
Shutterstock: 1b Eric Isselée, 2b Anke van Wyk, 3r worldswildlifewonders, 4l Thierry Maffeis, 5b Nickolay Stanev, 6 JustASC, 7 kristian sekulic, 8b Vladyslav Morozov, 9 Tan Kian Khoon, 10l mountainpix, 11 Rich Koele, 12 Stefanie van der Vinden, 13t, 13b urosr, 15b Four Oaks, 15t Martin Vrlik, 16 Dvoretskiy Igor Vladimirovich, 17b Gerard Lazaro, 17t Dmytro Korolov, 18l Craig Dingle, 19t Christopher Meder – Photography, 20l Anke van Wyk, 21b Michael Lynch., 26l Braam Collins, 26tr palko 72, 26bl Chris Pole, 26br Karen Givens, 27tl Ivan Kuzmin, 27tr palko 72, 27bl Anan Kaewkhammul, 27br s1001, 28tl irabel8, 28tr dirkr, 28bl Christian Musat, 28br Susan Flashman, 29 tl David Young, 29bl Michael Lynch, 29br Helen E. Gross, 30tl Nick Biemans, 30tr Prochasson Frederic, 30bl Emmanuel R Lacoste, 30br Dan Rodney, 31 tl Hung Chung Chih, 31tr Sharp photos, 31bl Henk Bentilage, 31br Ewan Chesser, 32b, 33c, 35b, 36, 37t, 37b, 38c, 38b, 39t, 40t, 40b, 41c, 42b, 43, 44t, 44b, 46, 46t, 47t, 50, 51c, 51r, 52tl piotrwzk, 52tr Steve Cukrov, 52bl Joyce Mar, 52br Jason Mintzer, 53tl, 53tr Igorsky, 53bl Tom Grundy, 53br luchschen, 54tl Chinnu4691, 54tr KKaplin, 54bl Alexander Chaikin, 54br Rusty Dodson, 55tl Dariusz Majgier, 55br Mikeledray, 56tr jele, 56tr Simon Gurney, 56bl Susan Flashman, 56br Maxim Petrichuk, 57tl idreamphoto 57tr Ryan M Bolton, 57bl arcimages, 57br Elisabeth Spencer, 58b pandapaw, 62t FloridaStock, 62b Reddogs, 63t H. Tuller, 64t JKlingebiel, 65t Eric Isselée, 66 Milena, 67r Eric Isselée, 67l Pichugin Dmitry, 68t pandapaw, 69t Jill Lang, 70t Luca Bertolli, 70b Brian Prawl, 71t Jaros, 72c Christian Musat, 73t M. Uptegrove, 74t John Carnemolla, 75t NSemprevivo, 76t Christian Wilkinson, 76b Reinhold Leitner, 77r Gentoo Multimedia Ltd, 78 tl K Kuliknov, 78tr lack-shot, 78bl Andy Dean Photography, 7br tomtsya, 79tl Achim Banque, 79tr ICI974, 79bl Florida Stock, 79br Kaido Kaerner, 80tl Yykkaa, 80tr Cloudia Newland, 80bl Chris Pole, 80br Prasit Chansaleekorn, 81tl mlorenz, 81tr Francis Bosse, 81bl Brian Upton, 81br Kathie M Thomas, 82tl Arthur van der Kooij, 82tr a9photo, 82bl Judy Kennamer, 82br Joanne Harris and Daniel Bubrich, 83tl Leksele, 83tr Lucky Business, 83 bl IF Stewart, 83br Gentoo Multimedia Ltd, 87t Eric Isselée, 90t Heather L. Jones, 92l Chen Wei Seng, 93t Studio 37, 94b kojik, 97t aida ricciardiello, 97b Geoff Hardy, 99t Ivanova Inga, 100t PBorowka, 100b Tyler Fox, 102l tubuceo, 103c kristian sekulic, 104tl P Borowka, 104tr Rostislav Ageev, 104 br Ian Scott, 105tr Stubblefield Photography, 105bl lavigne herve, 105br Vanillafire, 106bl Ivanova Inga, 106br Roman & Olexandra, 107bl Rich Carey, 108 tl Vladimir Wrangel, 108 tr Cigdem Cooper, 108bl 2009fotofriends, 109tl Mindstorm, 109bl Alta Oosthuizen, 109br Undersea Discoveries
SPL 42t, 48, 93b Paul Zahl
stock.xchange pp84-109 (coral borders) Swandieve & hirekatsu, 88t 93t 97b 100b porah, 87t, 99b satty4u
Stock Xchange 34, pp 58-83 TouTouke & straymuse, 62b 67l 68b 73t 75t 76b porah, 69b 70b 73b satty 60u

The words in **bold** are explained in the Glossary on page 112.

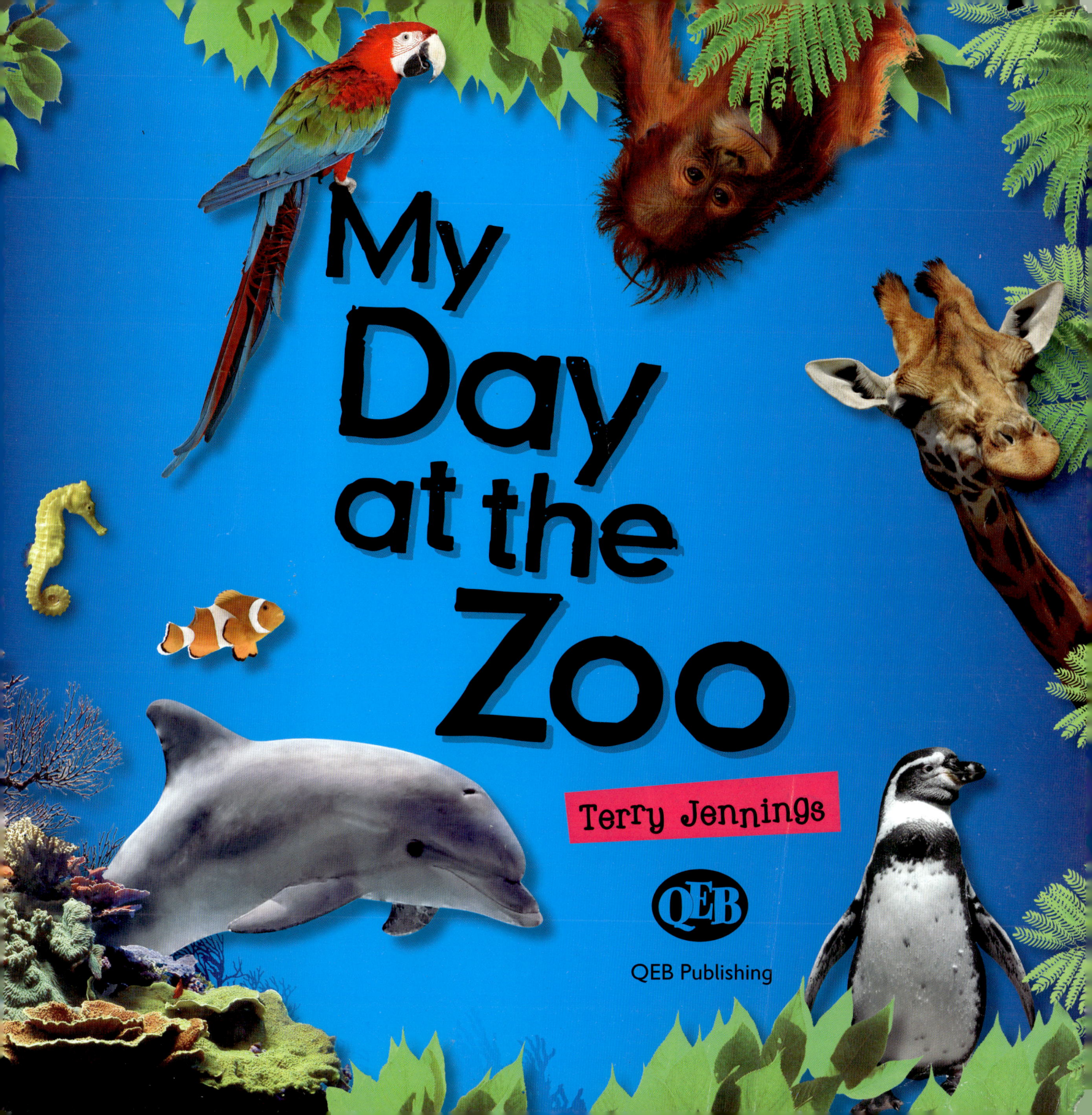

My Day at the Zoo

Terry Jennings

QEB Publishing

Contents

Mammal Kingdom

Who Lives in the
  Mammal Kingdom? . 8
Lions 10
Tigers 12
Giraffes 14
Zebras 16
Elephants 18
Camels 20
Kangaroos 22
Monkeys 24
Spotter's Guide . . . 26

Reptile Park

Reptile Parks 34
Cobras and Other
  Snakes 36
Rattlesnakes 38
Crocodiles 40
Alligators 42
Lizards 44
Chameleons 46
Tortoises 48
Turtles and Terrapins . 50
Spotter's Guide . . . 52

Bird Paradise

Birds and Bird Parks . 60
Eagles 62
Vultures 64
Parrots 66
Peacocks 68
Flamingos and Storks . 70
Pelicans 72
Ostriches 74
Penguins 76
Spotter's Guide . . . 78

Amazing Aquarium

What is an Aquarium? 86
Sharks 88
Flat Fish 90
Sea Horses 92
Eels 94
Crabs and Lobsters . 96
Octopuses and Squid 98
Corals 100
Dolphins 102
Spotter's Guide . . 104

My Day at the Zoo . 110
Glossary 112
Index 116
Notes for Parents
 and Teachers . . 120

- 🐾 Which animal has humps on its back?
- 🐾 Why do lions yawn?
- 🐾 How does a giraffe drink from a puddle?

Who Lives in the Mammal Kingdom?

Today I am going to a safari park. Animals such as lions and zebras live in zoos and safari parks. These types of animal belong to the mammal kingdom.

↑ All mammals feed their babies on milk when they are young.

A **mammal** is an animal that has hair or fur and is fed with milk from its mother's body. Many common animals, such as dogs, are mammals. Human beings are also a type of mammal.

Zoo watch

■ ELEPHANT HABITAT

ENDANGERED

The map shows where in the world the animal is from. Information about the most rare or at risk animals is given when you see the **endangered** symbol.

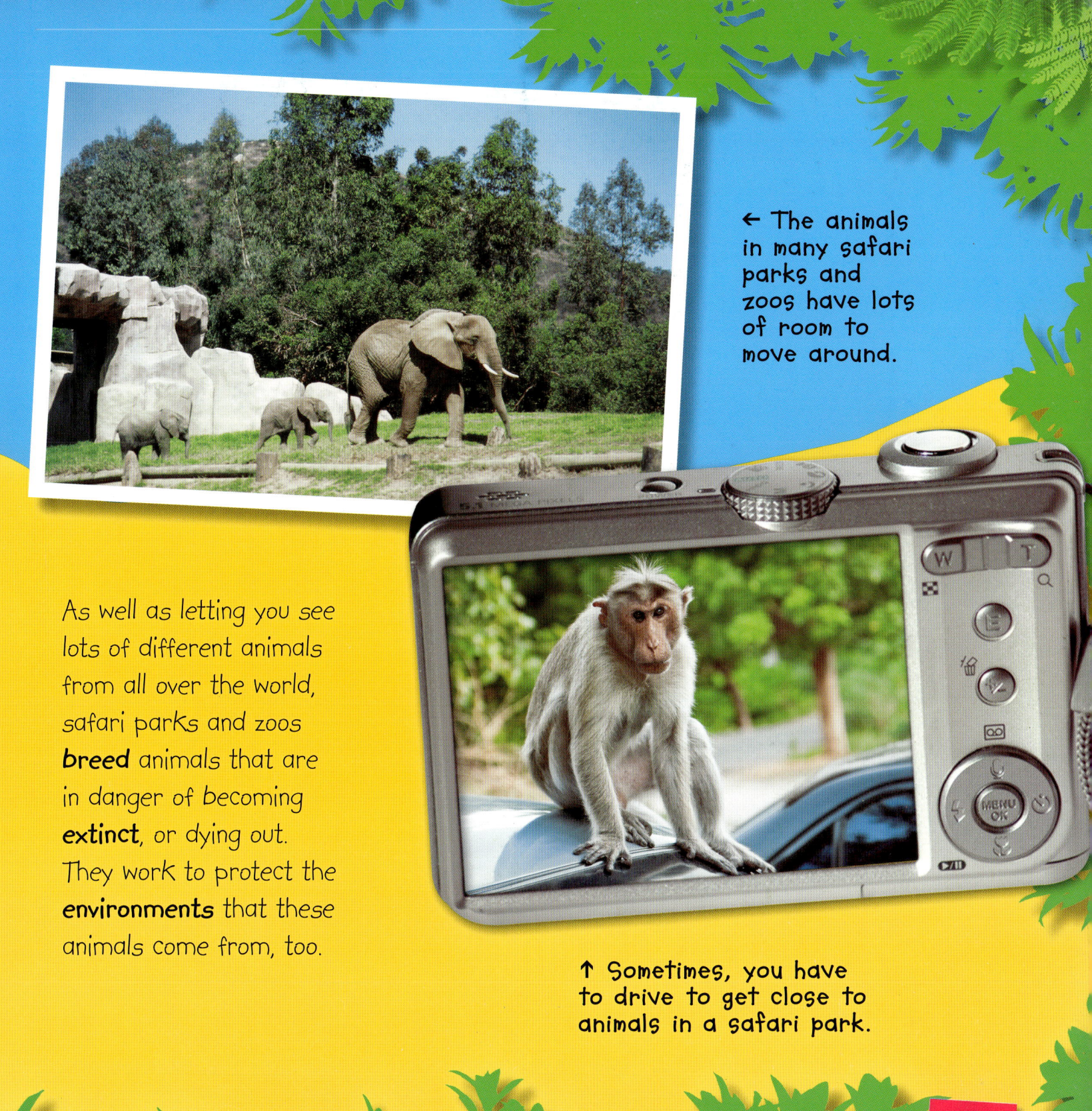

← The animals in many safari parks and zoos have lots of room to move around.

As well as letting you see lots of different animals from all over the world, safari parks and zoos **breed** animals that are in danger of becoming **extinct**, or dying out. They work to protect the **environments** that these animals come from, too.

↑ Sometimes, you have to drive to get close to animals in a safari park.

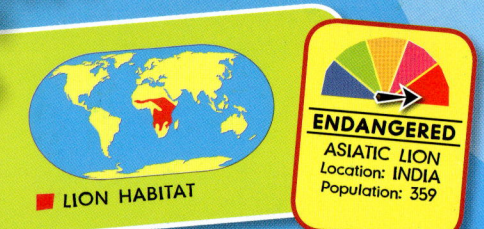

LION HABITAT

ENDANGERED
ASIATIC LION
Location: INDIA
Population: 359

Lions

At the safari park, I saw a pride of lions. They are part of the big cat family.

↑ A pride of lions. The male lion is the one with the long dark hair around his head and neck.

Male lions have a large, shaggy **mane** around their neck. Female lions are called lionesses. Their babies are called cubs.

ZOO VIEW

In the 1940s, there were about 400,000 lions in the world. Now there may be as few as 20,000. The National Geographic Society of America is helping save lions and other big cats from becoming extinct.

Although lions are a kind of cat, they cannot purr.
Instead, they roar to tell other lions where they are.
In Africa and India, lions hunt and kill other animals.
In safari parks, lions are fed on meat.

→ Lions yawn when they are tired, just like humans do.

Tigers

TIGER HABITAT

ENDANGERED
SIBERIAN TIGER
Location: SIBERIA
Population: 350-450

Tigers are the biggest of all cats. They are even bigger than lions. Tigers come from the forests and grasslands of Asia.

Tigers have striped coats, which helps them be **camouflaged**, or hidden, in the grass and trees when they hunt **prey**. In safari parks, tigers are fed big pieces of meat, which they tear up with their long, sharp teeth.

↑ A tiger's striped coat makes it very hard to spot when it is standing in long grass.

→ Tigers can eat so much meat at one meal that they may be fed only every few days.

Tigers are good swimmers. I saw a tiger make a big splash when it jumped into a pool in its **enclosure**.

→ Tigers like to cool off in water.

ZOO VIEW

In December 2008, 17 children, called the International Tiger Kids, stood by the tiger cage at the National Zoo in Washington DC. They were there to ask world leaders to help stop tigers from becoming extinct.

GIRAFFE HABITAT

ENDANGERED
GIRAFFES
Location: AFRICA
Population: less than 100,000

Giraffes

Giraffes are the world's tallest animals. They come from Africa. Their long necks help them reach leaves on the top of tall trees on which they feed.

The giraffe's spotted coat helps it hide from lions and other animals. Some giraffes have spotty coats, while others have patches. Giraffes' coats are never exactly alike.

→ A giraffe's tongue is about 16 inches (40 centimeters) long.

↑ The giraffe's height helps it see enemies from far away.

Three things
you didn't know about...
GIRAFFES

1 Although a giraffe's neck is nearly 6 feet (2 meters) long, it only has seven bones—that's the same number of bones as in your neck!

2 A giraffe's tongue is dark blue.

3 Giraffes usually stand up when they sleep. If they slept lying down, it would take them too long to get up if a **predator**, or enemy, came near.

At the safari park, I watched a giraffe drinking. Its front legs were so long that it had to spread them wide apart to get close enough to the ground to drink from a pool.

→ A giraffe has to bend down a long way to drink!

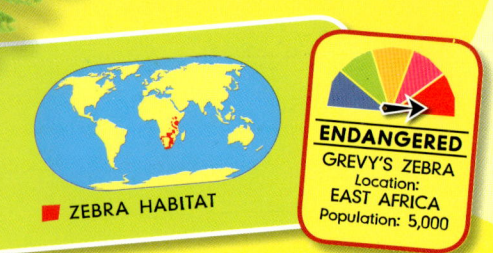

ZEBRA HABITAT

ENDANGERED
GREVY'S ZEBRA
Location:
EAST AFRICA
Population: 5,000

Zebras

Zebras come from the grasslands of Africa. They live in large groups, called herds.

A zebra's striped coat makes it hard for its enemies to see it. Zebras can run very fast—they can reach speeds of more than 40 miles (65 kilometers) per hour.

↓ In the wild, zebras can live for up to 25 years.

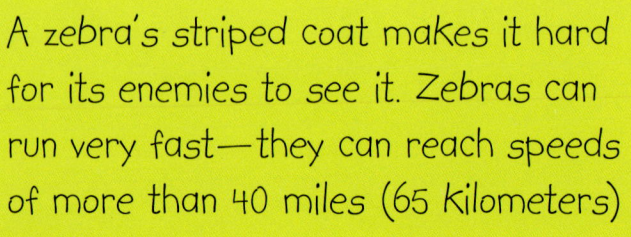

← In Africa, zebras live in large **herds** so that they can help each other watch out for danger.

In the safari park, I saw two zebras using their teeth to pick grass out of each other's fur. This is called **grooming**.

★ ZOO STARS

In April 2004, **rangers** in a **national park** in Nairobi, Kenya, discovered a baby zebra that had no stripes—the little zebra was white all over.

↑ Zebras groom each other's fur using their teeth.

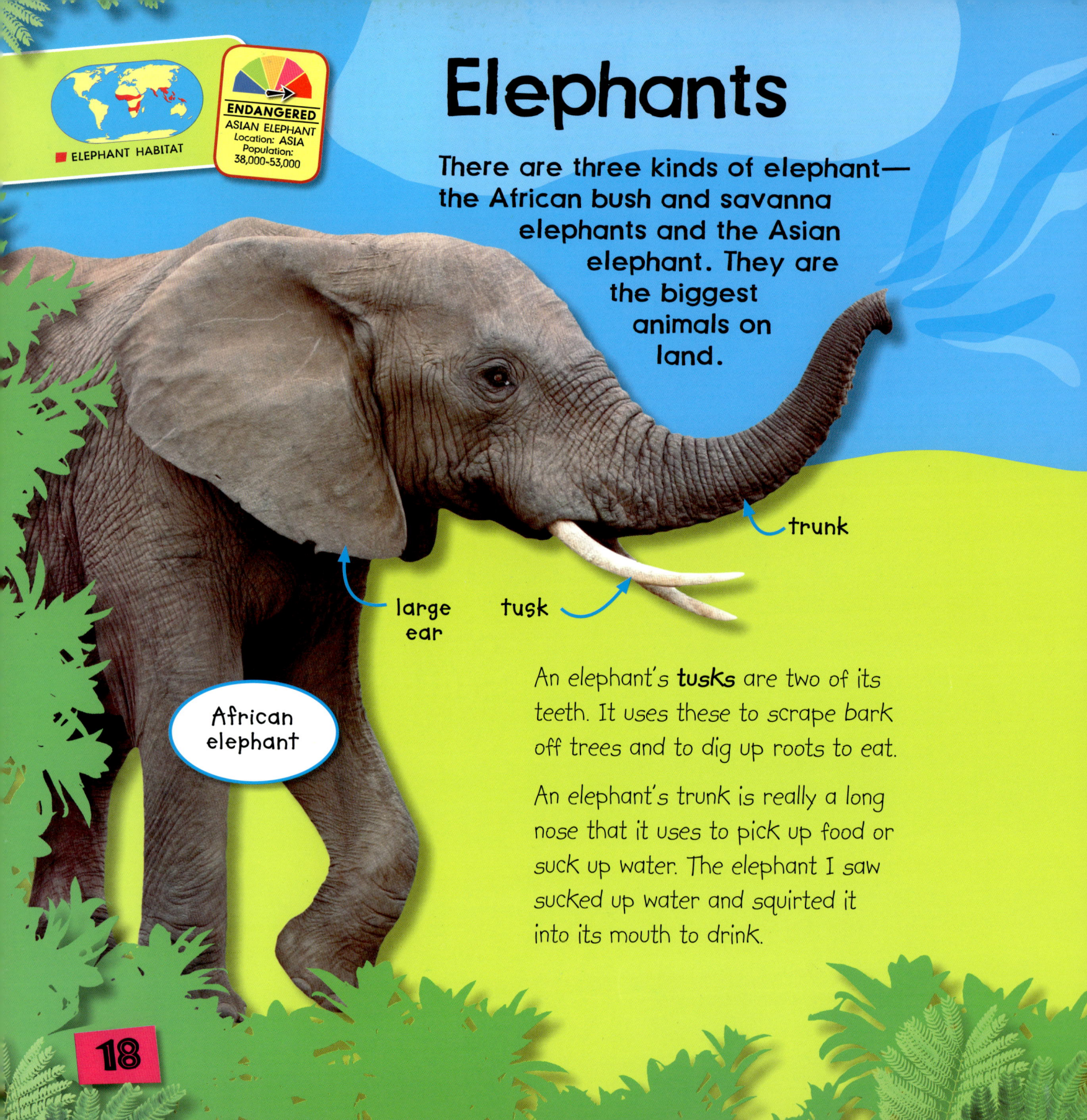

ELEPHANT HABITAT

ENDANGERED
ASIAN ELEPHANT
Location: ASIA
Population: 38,000–53,000

Elephants

There are three kinds of elephant—the African bush and savanna elephants and the Asian elephant. They are the biggest animals on land.

trunk

tusk

large ear

African elephant

An elephant's **tusks** are two of its teeth. It uses these to scrape bark off trees and to dig up roots to eat.

An elephant's trunk is really a long nose that it uses to pick up food or suck up water. The elephant I saw sucked up water and squirted it into its mouth to drink.

→ Asian elephants have smaller ears than African elephants.

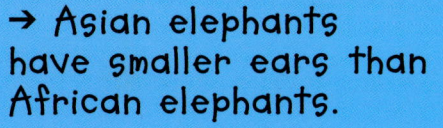

small ear

Asian elephant

← Baby elephants are called calves. They feed on their mother's milk until they are about four years old.

ZOO VIEW

In 2009, a herd of African elephants was damaging farmers' crops in Malawi. A conservation group called the International Fund for Animal Welfare, or IFAW, moved the elephants away from the crops to help the farmers.

Camels

Camels live in the world's hottest deserts. They have either one or two humps on their back.

WILD BACTRIAN CAMEL HABITAT

ENDANGERED
WILD BACTRIAN CAMEL
Location: ASIA
Population: 950

humps

Bactrian camel

There are two kinds of camel—the Arabian camel and the Bactrian camel. The camels I saw were Bactrian camels, which come from Asia. They have two humps.

← A camel has wide feet to stop it from sinking in the desert sand.

Arabian camels

The Arabian camel has one hump. It lives in North Africa, the Middle East, and India. The hump contains fat, which helps camels survive when they cannot find food or water in the **desert**.

↑ People use Arabian camels to carry them and their goods across deserts.

Three things you didn't know about... CAMELS

1. Arabian camels can drink 36 gallons (135 liters) of water in only 13 minutes.

2. Camels can run at speeds of more than 37 miles (60 kilometers) an hour.

3. Camels move two legs on one side of their body then two legs on the other when they run.

↑ A camel has two rows of eyelashes to protect its eyes in a sandstorm.

Kangaroos

KANGAROO HABITAT

ENDANGERED
RUFOUS HARE WALLABY
Location: AUSTRALIA
Population: 4,000

Gray kangaroo

Kangaroos and their close relatives wallabies come from Australia. In the wild, they can live in mobs, or groups, of more than 50 kangaroos or wallabies.

When a baby kangaroo is born, it crawls up into a **pouch** on its mother's belly. It stays there until it is big enough to come out, which can take more than nine months. The baby kangaroo I saw was peeping out of its mother's pouch.

← This female gray kangaroo is carrying a baby in her pouch.

Kangaroos leap along on their strong back legs. They use their large tail to **balance** when they are standing up.

↑ A kangaroo stretches out its tail when it jumps to help it keep its balance.

Red kangaroo

↑ The red kangaroo is the world's largest kangaroo.

Three things
you didn't know about...
KANGAROOS

1 Young kangaroos are called joeys.

2 Kangaroos cannot move backward.

3 When it is born, a baby kangaroo looks like a tiny pink worm. It would fit inside a teaspoon.

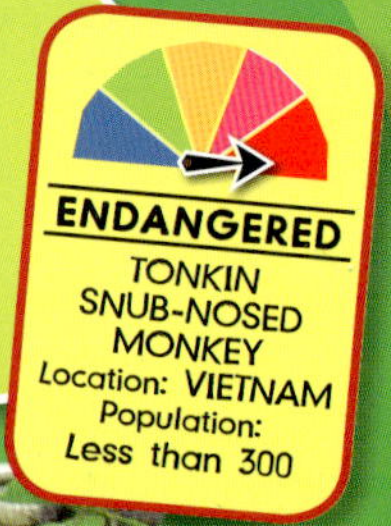

Monkeys

Most monkeys spend a lot of time in the trees, so they need to be good at climbing. Monkeys use their arms and legs to swing through the trees.

SPIDER MONKEY HABITAT

ENDANGERED
TONKIN SNUB-NOSED MONKEY
Location: VIETNAM
Population: Less than 300

strong tail

← This spider monkey from South America uses its strong tail to hold onto branches.

The monkeys I saw were vervet monkeys. They ran down onto the cars driving around the safari park to look at the people inside.

↑ Monkeys like looking at their reflection in car windows or mirrors.

24

When baby monkeys are born, they are carried by their mother for about two months, until they are old enough to look after themselves.

↑ There are up to 300 kinds of monkey in the world. This is a vervet monkey from Africa.

ZOO STARS

In Brazil, brown capuchin monkeys crack open the shell of a nut using a pebble. They put the nut on a large stone, then drop the pebble onto it to crack the shell.

↑ The pygmy marmoset is the world's smallest monkey. It is about the size of an adult's hand.

Spotter's Guide

LION

LENGTH **5.6–8.2 ft (1.7–2.5 m)**
WEIGHT **333.5–551 lb (150–250 kg)**
HABITAT **Africa and South Asia**

AFRICAN ELEPHANT

LENGTH **13–16 ft (4–5 m)**
WEIGHT **4.1–7.1 tons (4–7 tonnes)**
HABITAT **Africa**

TIGER

LENGTH **4.5–10.2 ft (1.4–3.1 m)**
WEIGHT **220–660 lb (100–300 kg)**
HABITAT **East Asia**

JAGUAR

LENGTH **5.2–5.4 ft (1.6–1.8 m)**
WEIGHT **66–220 lb (30–100 kg)**
HABITAT **Central to northern South America**

Quiz
How can you tell an African from an Asian elephant?

Answer: By the size of their ears.

GIRAFFE

LENGTH 13.8–17 ft (4.2–5.2 m)
WEIGHT 0.8–1.2 tons (0.8–1.2 tonnes)
HABITAT **Africa**

BURCHELL'S ZEBRA

LENGTH 7.2–8.2 ft (2.2–2.5 m)
WEIGHT 381–848 lb (175–385 kg)
HABITAT **East and southern Africa**

ASIAN ELEPHANT

LENGTH 18–21 ft (5.5–6.4 m)
WEIGHT 3–5.1 tons (3–5 tonnes)
HABITAT **South and Southeast Asia**

ARABIAN CAMEL

LENGTH 7.2–11.6 ft (2.2–3.4 m)
WEIGHT 990–1212 lb (450–550 kg)
HABITAT **Africa**

BACTRIAN CAMEL

LENGTH 8.2–9.2 ft (2.5–3 m)
WEIGHT 990–1520 lb (450–690 kg)
HABITAT **East Asia**

GRAY KANGAROO

LENGTH 2.3–5.9 ft (0.9–1.8 m)
WEIGHT 39.7–209 lb (18–95 kg)
HABITAT **South Australia**

RED KANGAROO

LENGTH 3.3–4.6 ft (1–1.4 m)
WEIGHT 55–198 lb (25–90 kg)
HABITAT **Australia**

PARMA WALLABY

LENGTH 17–20 in (45–53 cm)
WEIGHT 7.7–13 lb (3.5–6 kg)
HABITAT **East Australia**

CENTRAL AMERICAN SPIDER MONKEY

LENGTH 15.7–24.8 in (40–63 cm)
WEIGHT 6.6–20 lb (3–9 kg)
HABITAT Southern Mexico and Central America

VERVET MONKEY

LENGTH 17.7–26 in (45–66 cm)
WEIGHT 6.6–20 lb (3–9 kg)
HABITAT African woodland

PYGMY MARMOSET

LENGTH 4.7–5.9 in (12–15 cm)
WEIGHT 3.5–4.4 oz (100–125 g)
HABITAT West South America

BROWN CAPUCHIN

LENGTH 12.6–22.4 in (32–57 cm)
WEIGHT 5.7–10 lb (2.6–4.5 kg)
HABITAT Central and South America

Quiz

Why do monkeys have such powerful tails?

Answer: To help them climb trees and balance.

CHIMPANZEE

LENGTH 24.8–39 in (63–99 cm)
WEIGHT 66–132 lb (30–60 kg)
HABITAT West to Central Africa

EASTERN GORILLA

LENGTH 4.3–5.9 ft (1.3–1.8 m)
WEIGHT 150–463 lb (68–210 kg)
HABITAT Central Africa

ORANGUTAN

LENGTH 3.6–4.6 ft (1.1–1.4 m)
WEIGHT 88–176 lb (40–80 kg)
HABITAT Southeast Asia

KOALA

LENGTH 26–32.3 in (65–82 cm)
WEIGHT 8.8–26 lb (4–12 kg)
HABITAT Eastern Australia

GIANT PANDA

LENGTH 5.2–6.2 ft (1.6–1.9 m)
WEIGHT 220–275 lb (100–125 kg)
HABITAT East Asia

SPOTTED HYENA

LENGTH 37–65 in (95–165 cm)
WEIGHT 143–190 lb (65–86 kg)
HABITAT West to East and southern Africa

RING-TAILED LEMUR

LENGTH 15.4–18 ft (39–46 cm)
WEIGHT 5.5–7.3 lb (2.5–3.3 kg)
HABITAT Madagascar

BLACK PANTHER

LENGTH 4.1–5.4 ft (1.25–1.65 m)
WEIGHT 50.7–198 lb (23–90 kg)
HABITAT Africa and Asia

Quiz

What do koalas eat?

Answer: Eucalyptus leaves.

- Which slow-moving reptile can live up to 150 years?
- Why do snakes have forked tongues?
- How do chameleons change the color of their skin?

Reptile Parks

We are going to a reptile park today. Reptiles are animals such as lizards, snakes, crocodiles, turtles, and tortoises.

→ Reptiles like this lizard have scaly skin.

Reptile watch

CROCODILE HABITAT

ENDANGERED

The map shows where in the world the animal groups live. Information about the most rare or at-risk animals is shown under the **endangered** symbol.

A reptile is an animal with dry, scaly skin. Reptiles are **cold-blooded** animals, so their bodies are at the same temperature as the area that they live in. Most reptiles in the wild live in warm places on land, and most lay eggs.

The animals in reptile parks are kept in **enclosures** where they have space to move around. Reptile parks also breed animals that are in danger of becoming **extinct**. Reptile parks and zoos work to protect the environment these animals come from, too.

→ The snakes and many other reptiles in a reptile park are safely behind glass.

← Some larger reptiles are in special enclosures from which they cannot escape.

Cobras and Other Snakes

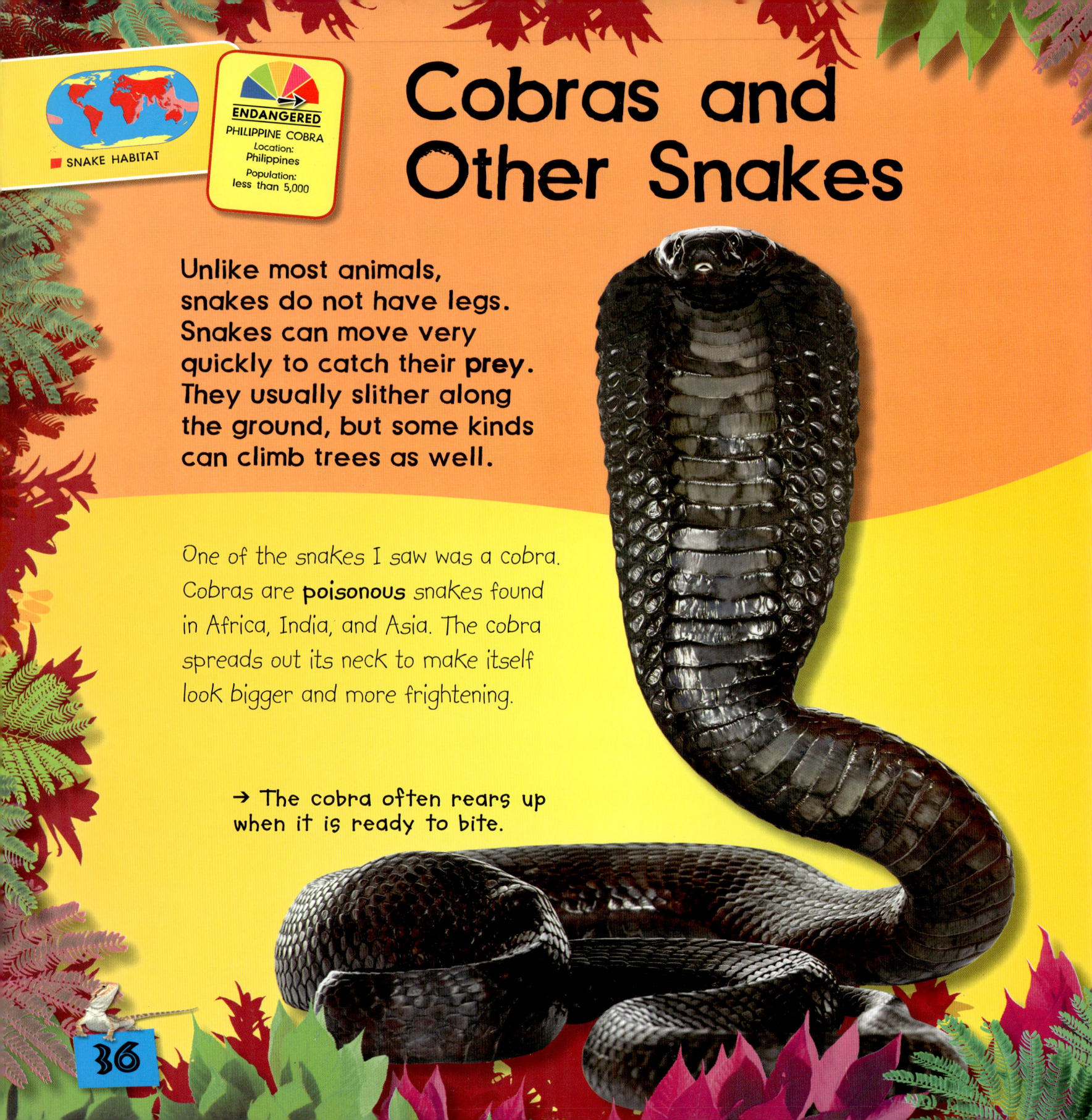

SNAKE HABITAT

ENDANGERED
PHILIPPINE COBRA
Location: Philippines
Population: less than 5,000

Unlike most animals, snakes do not have legs. Snakes can move very quickly to catch their **prey**. They usually slither along the ground, but some kinds can climb trees as well.

One of the snakes I saw was a cobra. Cobras are **poisonous** snakes found in Africa, India, and Asia. The cobra spreads out its neck to make itself look bigger and more frightening.

→ The cobra often rears up when it is ready to bite.

In another tank was a boa constrictor. Boa constrictors do not have poisonous **fangs**. Instead, they coil their body around prey and squeeze it to death.

→ This common boa can grow to be 13 feet (4 meters) long. It squeezes its prey to death.

↑ Snakes can shed their skin up to eight times in one year.

ZOO STARS

One reason why some reptiles face extinction is because they are taken from the wild and sold as pets. In 2009, a man was arrested at an airport in Norway. He had 14 royal pythons and 10 geckos taped to his body. He had hoped to sell them!

■ RATTLESNAKE HABITAT

ENDANGERED
ARUBA ISLAND RATTLESNAKE
Location: Aruba Island, Caribbean
Population: 230

Rattlesnakes

Rattlesnakes are found in North and South America. They are named after the rattling noise they make with their tail, which warns other animals they are poisonous.

↓ The western diamondback rattlesnake opens its mouth very wide, stabbing its fangs into its victim.

fangs

There are about 30 different kinds of rattlesnake. I saw a western diamondback rattlesnake at the reptile park. Rattlesnakes find their prey by smelling with their forked tongue, not their **nostrils**. Rattlesnakes feed on small animals, such as mice.

At the end of the rattlesnake's tail are some hard, loose pieces of skin. They are made of the same material as your fingernails. It is this skin that produces the rattling sound when the angry or frightened snake wags its tail.

forked tongue

rattle

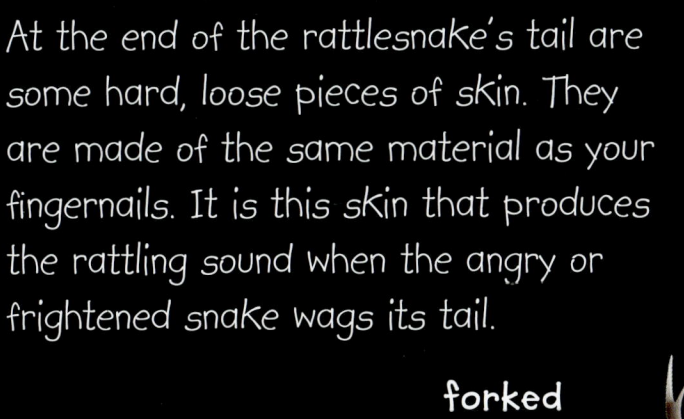

↓ This rattlesnake uses its forked tongue to smell its prey.

← The rattlesnake's rattle is at the tip of its tail.

ZOO VIEW

In Canada, many rattlesnakes are killed because people are afraid of being bitten by them. Toronto Zoo is teaching country people how to move rattlesnakes safely to areas where they can live undisturbed.

CROCODILE HABITAT

ENDANGERED
SIAMESE CROCODILE
Location: Cambodia
Population: Less than 250

Crocodiles

Crocodiles live in rivers and lakes in hot countries. They eat anything from fish and birds to large animals such as gazelles.

Crocodiles are very large reptiles. One of the Nile crocodiles I saw was nearly 20 feet (6 meters) long. Crocodiles lie in the river with only their eyes and nostrils showing above the water, waiting for prey to come to the river to drink. Then they grab it in their huge **jaws**.

eye — nostril

↑ Like most crocodiles, the Nile crocodile has eyes and nostrils on top of its head, so it can see and breathe in water.

→ This Nile crocodile shows its sharp teeth as it opens its mouth to stay cool.

teeth

The female crocodile guards her eggs and looks after the babies when they hatch.

Three things you didn't know about... CROCODILES

1 The largest crocodile in the world is a saltwater crocodile found from India to Southeast Asia and Australia. It can grow to be 23 feet (7 meters) long and weigh 1 ton (1 tonne).

2 Crocodiles can grasp and crush food with their teeth, but not chew it. Crocodiles have to swallow stones to help grind up the food in their stomach.

3 99 percent of baby crocodiles are eaten by predators during the first year of life.

↑ A female crocodile lays between 16 and 80 eggs in a hole dug in the riverbank.

ALLIGATOR HABITAT

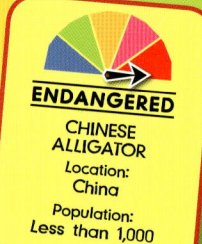
ENDANGERED
CHINESE ALLIGATOR
Location: China
Population: Less than 1,000

Alligators

There are only two kinds of alligator in the world—the American alligator and the Chinese alligator.

American alligators look very similar to crocodiles. The American alligator I saw looked just like a log until it moved. When it gets dark, alligators slide into the water and spend the night hunting. They eat fish and bigger animals, such as birds.

↑ Adult American alligators are black.

→ American alligator babies have yellow stripes.

A female alligator lays up to 60 eggs in a nest made of plants and mud. She digs the nest open when she hears the babies hatching. She looks after the young alligators for up to three years.

↓ The female American alligator carries her babies to safety in her mouth.

baby about 10 days old

← The Chinese alligator is now very rare.

ZOO VIEW

Until recently, there were fewer than 150 Chinese alligators left in the wild. The Wildlife Conservation Society released Chinese alligators that had been **bred** in American zoos into the Yangtze River in China to help breeding. This stopped the Chinese alligator from becoming extinct in the wild.

Lizards

LIZARD HABITAT

ENDANGERED
KOMODO DRAGON (A LIZARD)
Location: Indonesia
Population: 5,000

Lizards look a bit like crocodiles, but are much smaller. Most lizards have four legs, sharp claws on their feet, and a long tail.

← The frilled lizard of Australia spreads out the collar on its neck to frighten away enemies.

Lizards usually live in warm countries. They need to heat up in the sun before they can move about because they are cold-blooded. Most lizards can move very quickly. The geckos I saw were climbing up the walls of their tanks.

sticky pads

↑ A gecko is a lizard that has sticky pads on its toes. It can even run upside down across a ceiling.

44

↓ The Gila monster has unusual bead-shaped scales. It eats eggs, birds, mice, frogs—and other lizards!

thick skin with scales

claw

tongue

One lizard I saw was called a Gila monster. In the wild, Gila monsters live in the North American deserts. Their bright-red and black markings show that they have a poisonous bite.

ZOO VIEW

In 2008, scientists working near the mouth of the Mekong River in Southeast Asia discovered 18 new species of reptile. The scientists are worried that these animals may soon become extinct. This is because sea levels are rising as the Earth becomes warmer. All of these 'new' reptiles could soon be flooded out.

CHAMELEON HABITAT

ENDANGERED
NGURU PYGMY CHAMELEON
Location: East Africa
Population: World's rarest — endangered

Chameleons

The chameleon is a lizard that lives in trees. Chameleons are unusual because they can change the color of their skin.

Chameleons change the color of their skin when they are angry or frightened. They also change color to match their surroundings, so that they are **camouflaged**, or hard to see. This stops them from being attacked by **predators**.

↑ The male panther chameleon can change from this color...

↑ ...to this color when he wants to attract a mate.

Chameleons generally eat insects such as flies, but larger chameleons can eat small birds and other lizards. There were some large flies in the cage of the Jackson's chameleon that I saw. When one came too close, the chameleon shot out its long tongue and caught the fly.

Three things you didn't know about... CHAMELEONS

1 The world's smallest chameleon is a *Brookesia* chameleon from Madagascar. It is only 1.2 inches (3.3 centimeters) long.

2 Chameleons can move each eye separately.

3 Most chameleons lay eggs. In a few kinds, the eggs hatch inside the mother's body.

↑ This Jackson's chameleon from East Africa is using its tail to hold onto a flower.

TORTOISE HABITAT

ENDANGERED
GALAPAGOS TORTOISE
Location: Galapagos Islands
Population: 9,000—10,000

Tortoises

Tortoises have a hard shell covering their soft body. They live in places with a warm climate, such as South America. Tortoises can live to be more than 150 years old.

↓ Galapagos tortoises have a large, knobbly shell.

4 feet (1.2 meters) long

Tortoises' shells are very heavy, so these reptiles can only move slowly. The tortoise that I saw was a Galapagos tortoise. This is the world's largest **species** of tortoise. It can grow to be 4 feet (1.2 meters) long and weigh up to 470 pounds (215 kilograms).

Tortoises eat grass and other leaves, as well as fruit. They have a mouth a bit like a bird's beak, but no teeth. Instead, they cut up their food with their sharp **jaws**. Tortoises lay their eggs on land.

↑ The Indian starred tortoise has star-shaped markings on its knobbly shell.

ZOO STARS

In June 2006, Harriet the tortoise celebrated her 175th birthday at a zoo in Australia. She weighed 330 pounds (150 kilograms) and was about the size of a dinner table. She died of old age a few months later.

↑ The desert tortoise from the southwest US and Mexico has shovel-shaped front feet.

Turtles and Terrapins

TURTLE AND TERRAPIN HABITAT

ENDANGERED
WESTERN SWAMP TURTLE
Location: Australia
Population: 130 in wild, 200 in zoos

Like tortoises, turtles and terrapins have shells. Turtles are found in fresh water and the ocean in the warmer parts of the world, such as Asia. Terrapins are smaller turtles that are found in fresh water, such as lakes and rivers.

Many turtles spend nearly all of their life in the sea. Only the female turtles ever return to land. They crawl up to the beach to lay their eggs. The females bury their eggs in a hole in the sand and then they return to the ocean.

↓ The loggerhead sea turtle can weigh as much as three people!

Like turtles, terrapins lay their eggs on land. Newborn terrapins are almost an inch (2 centimeters) long. Within three years, terrapins will grow to about 5 inches (12 centimeters) long. Terrapins can live for 70 years.

← This terrapin is laying her eggs in a hole in the sand on a beach.

ZOO STARS

In 2009, a group called the Animal Guardians Association took a turtle with a broken shell to a hospital for treatment in Thailand. The doctors made a pretend shell to fit over its shell. This shell will fall off when the real shell is healed.

↑ Newly hatched baby turtles face many dangers as they crawl down the beach toward the ocean.

Spotter's Guide

NILE CROCODILE

LENGTH 11.5–19.7 ft (3.5–6 m)
WEIGHT 485–2000 lb (220–900 kg)
HABITAT Africa, Madagascar

AMERICAN CROCODILE

LENGTH Up to 15 ft (4.6 m)
WEIGHT Up to 1 ton (1 tonne)
HABITAT Central American coasts

SALTWATER CROCODILE

LENGTH 16–19.7 ft (5–6 m)
WEIGHT 1300 lb–1 ton (600 kg – 1 tonne)
HABITAT Southeast Asia

EGYPTIAN COBRA

LENGTH 3.5–8.2 ft (1–2.5 m)
WEIGHT Up to 19.8 lb (9 kg)
HABITAT North, West and East Africa

Quiz

How does the western diamondback warn predators?

Answer: With its rattle!

BOA CONSTRICTOR

LENGTH **3.5–13 ft (1–4 m)**
WEIGHT **Up to 60 lb (27 kg)**
HABITAT **On land or trees in Central and South America and Caribbean**

ROYAL PYTHON

LENGTH **2.6–3.9 ft (0.8–1.2 m)**
WEIGHT **3.3 lb (1.5 kg)**
HABITAT **West to Central Africa**

WESTERN DIAMONDBACK

LENGTH **Up to 6.6 ft (2 m)**
WEIGHT **5.5–7.3 lb (2.5–3.3 kg)**
HABITAT **South USA and north Mexico**

AMERICAN ALLIGATOR

LENGTH **9.2–16.4 ft (2.8–5 m)**
WEIGHT **Up to 1 ton (1 tonne)**
HABITAT **Southeast USA**

CHINESE ALLIGATOR

LENGTH 4.9 ft (1.5 m)
WEIGHT 88 lb (40 kg)
HABITAT Yangtze River, China

FRILLED LIZARD OF AUSTRALIA

LENGTH 23.6–39.4 in (60–90 cm)
WEIGHT 1.1 lb (1.5 kg)
HABITAT South New Guinea and North Australia

COMMON HOUSE GECKO

LENGTH 4.7–5.9 in (12–15 cm)
WEIGHT 0.6 oz (18 g)
HABITAT Tropical regions worldwide

GILA MONSTER

LENGTH 13.8–19 in (35–50 cm)
WEIGHT 5.1 lb (2.3 kg)
HABITAT Southwest USA and north Mexico

Quiz

Do you know which chameleon is the most colorful?

Answer: The panther chameleon.

CHAMELEON OUSTALETS

LENGTH 19.7–26.8 in (50–68 cm)
WEIGHT 2–4 lb (0.9–2 kg)
HABITAT Madagascar

PANTHER CHAMELEON

LENGTH 15.7–20.3 in (40–52 cm)
WEIGHT 5.3–8.8 oz (150–250 g)
HABITAT Reunion Island, east and north Madagascar

BROOKESIA CHAMELEON

LENGTH 1.3 in (33 mm)
WEIGHT 0.01 oz (0.5 g)
HABITAT Madagascar

JACKSON'S CHAMELEON

LENGTH 7.9–11.8 in (20–30 cm)
WEIGHT 9.2 oz (260 g)
HABITAT East Africa and Hawaii

GALAPAGOS TORTOISE

LENGTH **Up to 4.9 ft (1.5 m)**
WEIGHT **Up to 1050 lb (475 kg)**
HABITAT **Galapagos islands on land**

GREEN TURTLE

LENGTH **3.3–3.9 ft (1–1.2 m)**
WEIGHT **250–450 lb (113–204 kg)**
HABITAT **Tropical and subtropical waters worldwide**

INDIAN STARRED TORTOISE

LENGTH **Up to 11 in (28 cm)**
WEIGHT **5.5 lb (2.5 kg)**
HABITAT **South Asia**

DESERT TORTOISE

LENGTH **9.8–14.2 (25–36 cm)**
WEIGHT **8.8–15 lb (4–7 kg)**
HABITAT **Southwest USA and north Mexico**

Quiz

How can turtles hide their head from predators?

Answer: By pulling it in or folding it under their shells.

LOGGERHEAD SEA TURTLE

LENGTH **27.6–39.4 in (70–100 cm)**
WEIGHT **197 lb (135 kg)**
HABITAT **Tropical and subtropical waters worldwide**

ALLIGATOR SNAPPING TURTLE

LENGTH **15.7–31.5 in (40–80 cm)**
WEIGHT **176 lb (80 kg)**
HABITAT **Tropical, subtropical, and temperate waters worldwide**

PAINTED TURTLE

LENGTH **5.4–9.8 in (15–25 cm)**
WEIGHT **28.2–31.7 oz (800–900 g)**
HABITAT **North America**

EASTERN BOX TURTLE

LENGTH **Up to 7.9 in (20 cm)**
WEIGHT **21.2–31.7 oz (600–900 g)**
HABITAT **Eastern USA**

- Which bird cracks open nuts and seeds with its beak?
- Why do flamingos live in a flock?
- How do birds of prey hunt for their food?

Birds and Bird Parks

Today we are going to a bird park. A bird park has lots of big cages called **aviaries** that the birds live in.

The birds in a bird park come from all over the world. Birds are the only animals that have feathers. All birds have a mouth called a **beak**, two legs, and two wings. Birds lay eggs with a shell, and most birds can fly.

Bird watch

■ PELICAN HABITAT

ENDANGERED

The map shows where in the world the animal is from. Information about the most rare or at-risk animals is given when you see the endangered symbol.

→ Inside a large aviary at a bird park.

Some of the aviaries in bird parks are so big you can walk through them. Many of the birds that live near water are out in the open where you can see them easily, while a few kinds wander around among the people. It's a bird paradise!

↑ Some birds in a bird park are able to walk around freely.

feathers

wing

beak

claws

→ Toucans have a very large beak.

tail

Eagles

■ EAGLE HABITAT

ENDANGERED
SERPENT EAGLE
Location: Madagascar
Population: Less than 250

Eagles are very large birds of prey. They live in mountains and forests all over the world.

American bald eagle

One of the biggest birds I saw was an American bald eagle. It had large feet with sharp claws, called **talons**. The bald eagle uses its feet to grab hold of prey and its beak to tear up food.

↑ The **wingspan** of an American bald eagle can be up to 7.8 feet (2.4 meters).

→ The American bald eagle has white feathers on its head and neck.

62

Another aviary I visited had a golden eagle in it. This eagle had a dark-brown back and pale head and neck. Golden eagles live in places where there are few people around, such as on mountains or on cliffs by the ocean.

golden eagle

→ Like all eagles, the golden eagle has very good eyesight.

ZOO VIEW

The white-tailed sea eagle is the fourth largest eagle in the world. It became extinct in the United Kingdom in 1918. In 1975, a few sea eagles were brought to an island off the coast of Scotland. They had chicks, and now there are more than 200 sea eagles in Scotland.

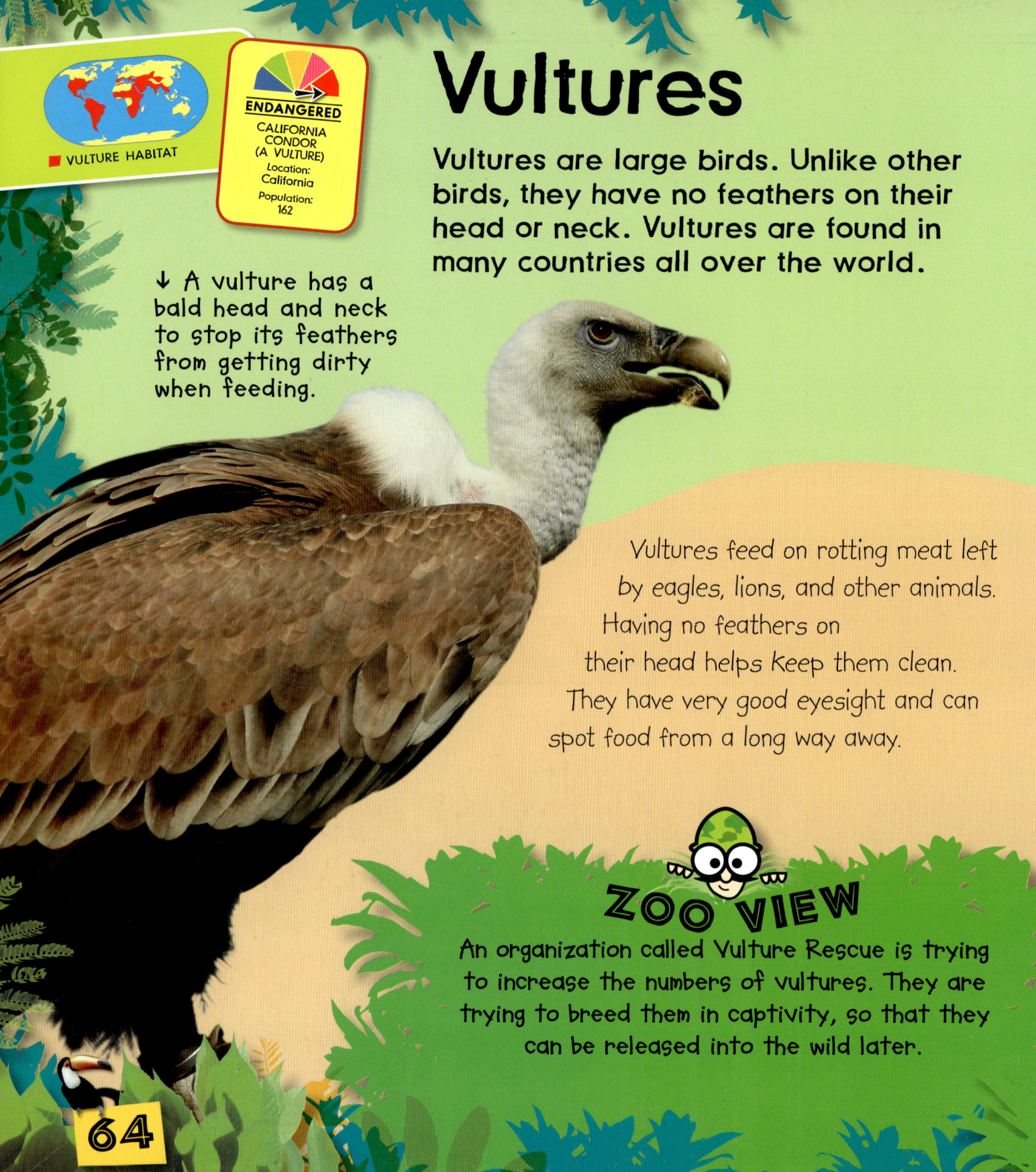

VULTURE HABITAT

ENDANGERED
CALIFORNIA CONDOR (A VULTURE)
Location: California
Population: 162

Vultures

Vultures are large birds. Unlike other birds, they have no feathers on their head or neck. Vultures are found in many countries all over the world.

↓ A vulture has a bald head and neck to stop its feathers from getting dirty when feeding.

Vultures feed on rotting meat left by eagles, lions, and other animals. Having no feathers on their head helps keep them clean. They have very good eyesight and can spot food from a long way away.

ZOO VIEW

An organization called Vulture Rescue is trying to increase the numbers of vultures. They are trying to breed them in captivity, so that they can be released into the wild later.

At the bird park, I learned that vultures do an important job because they clean up bodies left by hunting animals. These bodies would otherwise attract flies and germs.

↑ Vultures use their large wings to fly around for hours, looking for dead animals.

→ These vultures feeding at a garbage dump are not fussy about what they eat.

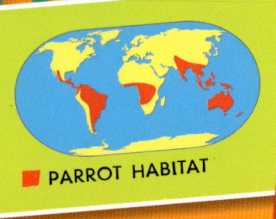
PARROT HABITAT

ENDANGERED
YELLOW-EARED PARROT
Location: Colombia
Population: Less than 125

Parrots

Parrots come from the warmer countries of the world, such as Australia.

Most parrots are brightly colored. The parrot I saw was a green-winged macaw from South America. It lives at the top of tall trees.

↑ The green-winged macaw feeds on fruits, seeds, and nuts.

Three things
you didn't know about...
PARROTS

1. There are 353 different species of parrot in the world.
2. Parrots can live for up to 80 years in the wild.
3. Many parrots can imitate, or copy, human voices.

There are many different species of parrot. Cockatoos are found in Australia. Lovebirds are small parrots from Africa and Madagascar. They get their name from the way they sit together in pairs, resting their heads against each other.

↓ African lovebirds like these ones are always found in pairs.

↓ In Australia, sulphur-crested cockatoos live in large flocks.

PEACOCK HABITAT

ENDANGERED
GREEN PEAFOWL
Location: Southeast Asia
Population: Less than 10,000

Peacocks

The peacocks at the bird park were walking around in the open, following the visitors.

Peacocks first came from Asia, but they have lived in parks and large gardens in Europe for thousands of years.

tail feathers

↑ The peacock has the longest tail feathers of any bird.

peahen

→ The peahen is a dull brown color. This makes her hard to see when sitting on her eggs.

babies

↑ The peacock can spread his tail out like a fan to attract a mate.

The male peacock has the longest tail feather of any kind of bird. The female (called a peahen) is a dull brown color. Although peacocks and peahens feed on the ground, they sleep high in trees at night, safe from most enemies.

ZOO STARS

Percy the peacock lives in a village in Lincolnshire, England. When Percy found a mate, he became a nuisance with his loud screeches. Now people in the village are arguing about whether he should stay!

ENDANGERED
PAINTED STORK
Location: Asia
Population: 25,000

Flamingos and Storks

Flamingos live in large groups on shallow lakes in Africa, South America, Asia, and southern Europe. Flamingos are a kind of **wading** bird.

Flamingos feed on shrimps and other water animals. They catch these by wading through water, moving their beak from side to side to sieve food from the water.

↑ Flamingos sieve tiny animals from the water with their specially shaped beak.

→ Flamingos stand on one leg for many hours at a time, even when they are asleep.

Storks are also wading birds. They spend the winter in Africa and in summer **migrate** to Europe to build their nests. At the bird park, I saw two storks sitting on a huge nest on a wooden platform in a tree. In some parts of Europe, storks nest on the chimneys of houses.

⭐ ZOO STARS

Two scientists in America studied flamingos to find out why they often stand on one leg. Eventually, the scientists found the answer—standing on one leg stops the flamingo's body losing too much heat. They swap legs to stop each leg becoming too cold.

↑ In some parts of Europe, white storks nest on house chimneys. Some people believe it is lucky to have storks nesting on your house.

Pelicans

■ PELICAN HABITAT

ENDANGERED
DALMATIAN PELICAN
Location: Eastern Europe and East-Central Asia
Population: 10,000–13,900

At the bird park, I saw some pelicans. They are large seabirds.

The pelican's beak has a huge **pouch** that holds three times as much as its stomach. It uses the pouch to scoop up fish from the water and also to collect water to drink. Fully stretched, the pouch can hold as much as a large pail.

pouch

← The pelican's pouch lets it eat a lot of food quickly.

72

The brown pelican of North and South America catches fish by diving into the ocean. American white pelicans work together to catch fish. They form a line and herd fish in front of them into the shallow water. There the fish are easy to catch.

↑ The pelican dives down to scoop up fish in the water.

↑ Baby pelicans take food from their mother's and father's beaks.

ZOO STARS

In 1976, a pelican called Mr. Percival from Adelaide Zoo, Australia, was the star of a film called "Storm Boy," which was about a boy who looks after pelicans.

OSTRICH HABITAT

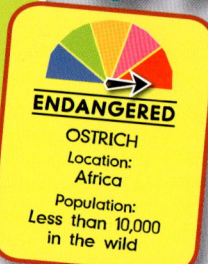
ENDANGERED
OSTRICH
Location: Africa
Population: Less than 10,000 in the wild

Ostriches

Not all birds can fly. Although they have small wings, the world's biggest birds—ostriches—cannot fly.

→ Although an ostrich cannot fly, it can run very fast from danger.

Three things you didn't know about... OSTRICHES

1. Most birds have four toes, but an ostrich has only two.

2. An ostrich has the largest eye of any land animal. It measures 2 inches (5 centimeters) across.

3. An ostrich's egg weighs about 3.7 pounds (1.7 kilograms).

Ostriches run at speeds of up to 43 miles (70 kilometers) per hour, which helps them escape enemies such as lions. Ostriches live on the dry grasslands of Africa.

Female ostriches lay their eggs in a nest on the ground. The eggs are the biggest of all birds. The male ostrich sits on the eggs to keep them warm at night. The female sits on the eggs during the day.

↑ The eggs of an ostrich are the largest of any bird.

← Male ostriches are black and white. They can grow to be 9 feet (2.8 meters) tall. The females are smaller and grayish-brown.

75

PENGUIN HABITAT

ENDANGERED
HUMBOLDT PENGUIN
Location: South America
Population: 3,000—12,000

Penguins

Penguins live near some of the world's coldest oceans. Penguins cannot fly, but they can swim better than any other bird.

Penguins swim using their small, stiff wings like paddles. They use their tail and feet for steering. While they are swimming, penguins hunt for fish and shrimp to eat.

← These Adelie penguins live among the ice and snow of Antarctica.

Adelie penguins

→ Penguins use their small, stiff wings to swim underwater in search of fish and shrimp.

76

The emperor penguin is the largest of all penguins. It can grow to 47 inches (120 centimeters) tall and weigh up to 74 pounds (37 kilograms).

In the winter, the female emperor penguin lays one egg. She then goes out to sea and doesn't return until spring. The male balances the egg on his feet to keep it warm. When the baby hatches, it stays close to its father for the first few weeks.

← 47 inches (120 centimeters) tall

Emperor penguin

↑ The emperor penguin does not build a nest. Instead, the male keeps his chick warm under a flap of skin on his stomach.

Three things
you didn't know about...
PENGUINS

1 There are at least 18 different kinds of penguin.

2 A penguin can hold its breath for about 20 minutes under water.

3 Penguins use a kind of sign language to "talk" to each other.

Spotter's Guide

GREEN WINGED MACAW

LENGTH 35 in (90 cm)
WEIGHT 42–60 oz (1.2–1.7 kg)
HABITAT North and central South America

BLUE AND YELLOW MACAW

LENGTH 35 in (90 cm)
WEIGHT 31–46 oz (900–1300 g)
HABITAT North and central South America

CALIFORNIAN CONDOR

LENGTH 3.9–4.3 ft (1.2–1.3 m)
WEIGHT 17–31 lb (8–14 kg)
HABITAT California and Arizona

TOUCAN

LENGTH 8–23 in (20–60 cm)
WEIGHT 19.4 oz (550 g)
HABITAT Northeast to central South America

Quiz

Which of these birds stands on one foot, even when it sleeps?

Answer: The Flamingo.

OSTRICH

LENGTH 6.0–8.9 ft (1.8–2.7 m)
WEIGHT 138–290 lb (63–130 kg)
HABITAT West to East Africa and South Africa

FLAMINGO

LENGTH 4.9 ft (1.5 m)
WEIGHT 8.8 lb (4 kg)
HABITAT South America, Caribbean, Southwest Europe, Asia, and Africa

AMERICAN BALD EAGLE

LENGTH 28–37.8 in (71–96 cm)
WEIGHT 6.6–14.3 lb (3–6.5 kg)
HABITAT North America

WHITE-TAILED SEA EAGLE

LENGTH 27.2–36.2 in (69–92 cm)
WEIGHT 6.8–11.9 lb (3.1–5.4 kg)
HABITAT Northern Europe and west Mediterranean

GOLDEN EAGLE

LENGTH 27.5–35.4 in (75–90 cm)
WEIGHT 6.6–14.3 lb (3–6.5 kg)
HABITAT North America, Europe, Asia, North Africa

GREEN PEAFOWL

LENGTH 5.9–7.5 ft (1.8–2.3 m)
WEIGHT 8.8–13.2 lb (4–6 kg)
HABITAT South Asia

SERPENT EAGLE

LENGTH 20.1–23.6 in (51–60 cm)
WEIGHT 2.6–4.4 lb (1.2–2 kg)
HABITAT Brunei, Indonesia, Malaysia

VULTURE

LENGTH 37 in (94 cm)
WEIGHT 8.8–15.4 lb (4–7 kg)
HABITAT Africa

BARN OWL

LENGTH 9.8–17.7 in (25–45 cm)
WEIGHT Up to 17.6 oz (500 g)
HABITAT Worldwide

GREAT HORNED OWL

LENGTH 18.1–26.8 in (46–68 cm)
WEIGHT 33.5 oz (1400 g)
HABITAT Americas

PALM COCKATOO

LENGTH 23.6 in (60 cm)
WEIGHT 2.2 lb (1 kg)
HABITAT New Guinea, Northeast Australia

SULPHUR-CRESTED COCKATOO

LENGTH 19.7 in (50 cm)
WEIGHT 33.5 oz (950 g)
HABITAT New Guinea, Australia

Quiz

Why are vultures bald?

Answer: To help keep their head clean when they eat.

COMMON KESTREL

LENGTH 12.6–15.4 in (32–39 cm)
WEIGHT 4.9–7.1 oz (140–200 g)
HABITAT North America, Europe, Asia, North Africa

BROWN PELICAN

LENGTH 39.4–53 in (100–137 cm)
WEIGHT 4.4–11 lb (2–5 kg)
HABITAT Americas

RAINBOW LORIKEET

LENGTH 9.8–11.8 in (25–30 cm)
WEIGHT 4.2–4.9 oz (120–140 g)
HABITAT Australia, Auckland, New Zealand, Asia

GOULDIAN FINCH

LENGTH 5.1–5.5 in (130–140 mm)
WEIGHT 0.5 oz (15 g)
HABITAT Australia

Quiz

How did the African lovebird get its name?

Answer: They usually sit together in pairs.

ATLANTIC PUFFIN

LENGTH 9.8 in (25 cm)
WEIGHT Up to 17.6 oz (500 g)
HABITAT North Pacific and Atlantic Ocean

AFRICAN LOVEBIRD

LENGTH 5.7 in (14.5 cm)
WEIGHT 1.8 oz (50 g)
HABITAT East Africa

ADELIE PENGUIN

LENGTH 18.1–29.5 in (46–75 cm)
WEIGHT 8.6–12.8 lb (3.9–5.8 kg)
HABITAT Antarctic Coast

EMPEROR PENGUIN

LENGTH 48 in (122 cm)
WEIGHT 48.5–99 lb (22–45 kg)
HABITAT Antarctica

- Which ocean creature only walks sideways?
- Why do squid squirt ink?
- How does a dolphin breathe air but live in the ocean?

What is an Aquarium?

We are going to an aquarium today. An aquarium is a large building containing tanks where fish and other water animals are kept for people to see.

↑ Aquariums often have tanks with many different kinds of fish.

Aquariums let you see lots of different fish and water animals from all over the world. They also breed creatures that are in danger of becoming extinct, or dying out. They work to protect the environments that these creatures live in, too.

tail
fins
eye
mouth
gill cover
scales

↑ Clownfish are popular fish to keep in an aquarium.

Fish are animals that live and breathe in water. Some tanks in aquariums have fresh water in them, where fish from lakes, ponds, and rivers live. Other tanks contain salt water, where fish and other animals from oceans and seas are kept.

Sea watch

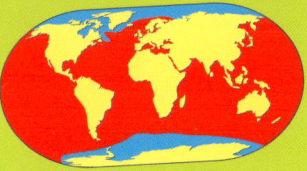
SHARK HABITAT

ENDANGERED

The map shows where in the world the animal is from. Information about the most rare or at-risk animals is given when you see the endangered symbol.

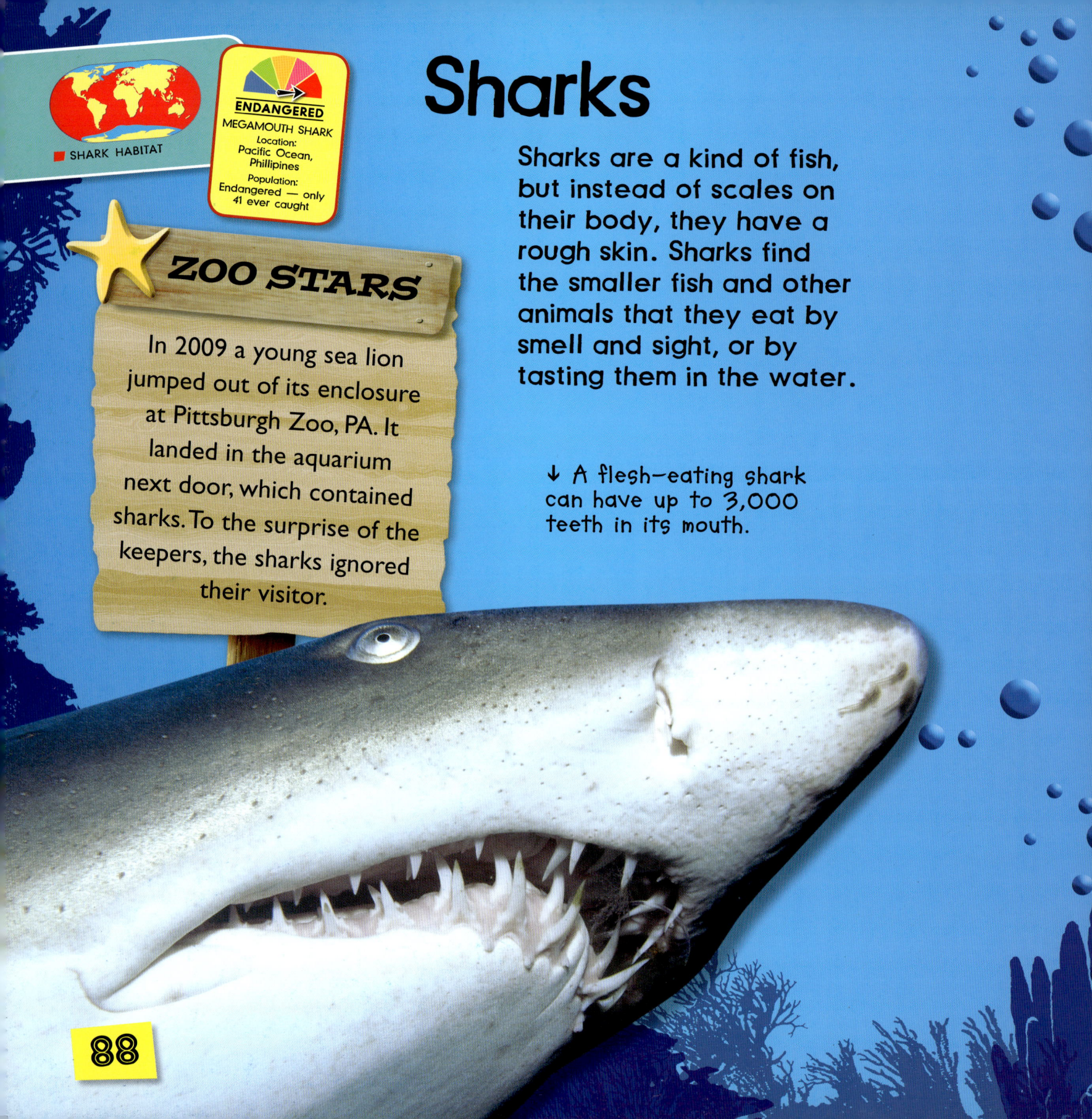

SHARK HABITAT

ENDANGERED
MEGAMOUTH SHARK
Location: Pacific Ocean, Phillipines
Population: Endangered — only 41 ever caught

Sharks

Sharks are a kind of fish, but instead of scales on their body, they have a rough skin. Sharks find the smaller fish and other animals that they eat by smell and sight, or by tasting them in the water.

↓ A flesh-eating shark can have up to 3,000 teeth in its mouth.

ZOO STARS

In 2009 a young sea lion jumped out of its enclosure at Pittsburgh Zoo, PA. It landed in the aquarium next door, which contained sharks. To the surprise of the keepers, the sharks ignored their visitor.

The smooth-hound sharks I saw were quite small, but some sharks are large. The biggest shark in the world is the whale shark, which can grow to more than 49 feet (15 meters) long and weigh up to 13.2 tons (13 tonnes)—that's as heavy as seven cars!

→ A hammerhead shark's eyes and nostrils are on the ends of its "hammer."

The funniest-looking sharks I saw were called hammerhead sharks. They have a huge, flat head with eyes at the sides of it.

← The whale shark can grow to more than 49 feet (15 meters). It eats tiny animals and plants.

MANTA RAY HABITAT

ENDANGERED
KLEIN'S SOLE
Location: Mediterranean
Population: Endangered — very rare

Flat Fish

Fish come in all shapes and sizes. Some fish, such as plaice and rays, have a thin, flat body.

Plaice are flat fish. In the wild, plaice live close to the ocean floor. They can hide from their enemies by changing color to blend in with the seabed. They swim on their sides.

← A flounder resting on sand.

→ A plaice buries itself in the sand to avoid being spotted by its enemies.

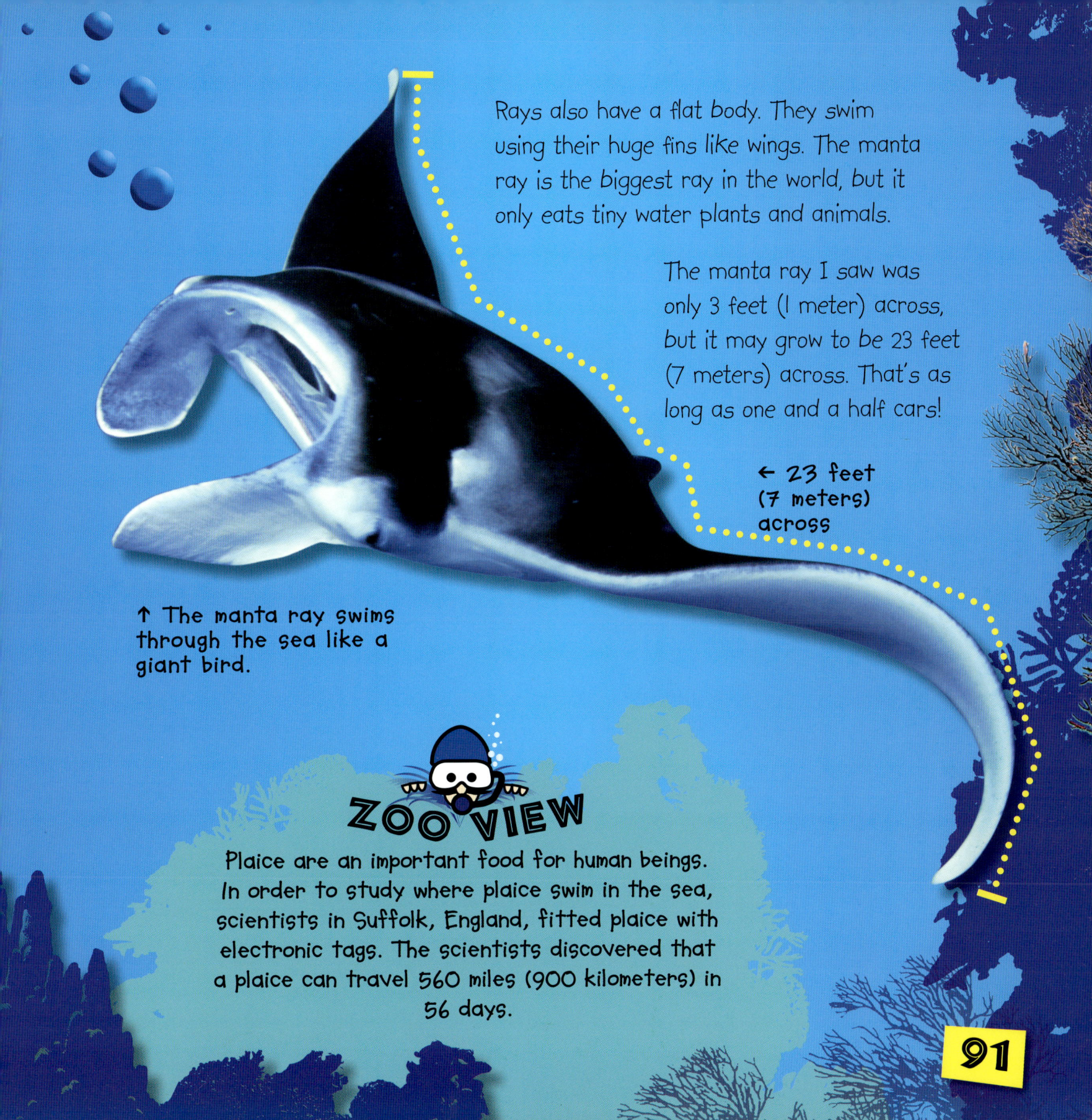

Rays also have a flat body. They swim using their huge fins like wings. The manta ray is the biggest ray in the world, but it only eats tiny water plants and animals.

The manta ray I saw was only 3 feet (1 meter) across, but it may grow to be 23 feet (7 meters) across. That's as long as one and a half cars!

← 23 feet (7 meters) across

↑ The manta ray swims through the sea like a giant bird.

ZOO VIEW

Plaice are an important food for human beings. In order to study where plaice swim in the sea, scientists in Suffolk, England, fitted plaice with electronic tags. The scientists discovered that a plaice can travel 560 miles (900 kilometers) in 56 days.

■ SEA HORSE HABITAT

ENDANGERED
KNYSNA SEA HORSE
Location: South Africa
Population: Endangered — world's rarest

Sea Horses

Sea horses are fish that live in warmer seas. They swim upright and are covered in bony plates. Sea horses are tiny—most species are no more than 11 inches (30 centimeters) high.

→ no more than 4 inches (10 centimeters) high

↑ The sea horse gets its name because it swims upright and its head looks like a horse's.

ZOO VIEW

More than 25 million sea horses are sold as pets or to be made into medicines each year. A chocolate company in Belgium is paying scientists to find out more about sea horses and how they can be saved.

The sea horses I saw spent most of the time with their tails curled around seaweed. They were eating tiny shrimp and water plants that floated by them.

baby sea horse

male sea horse

↑ Sea horses use their tails to hang on to weeds, not for swimming. They swim by waving their tiny fins.

When a female sea horse lays eggs, she puts them into a little pouch on the belly of the male sea horse. Between 10 days and 6 weeks later, more than 200 tiny sea horses hatch from the eggs and swim away from their father.

↑ The sea horse is the only animal in the world in which the male gives birth to babies.

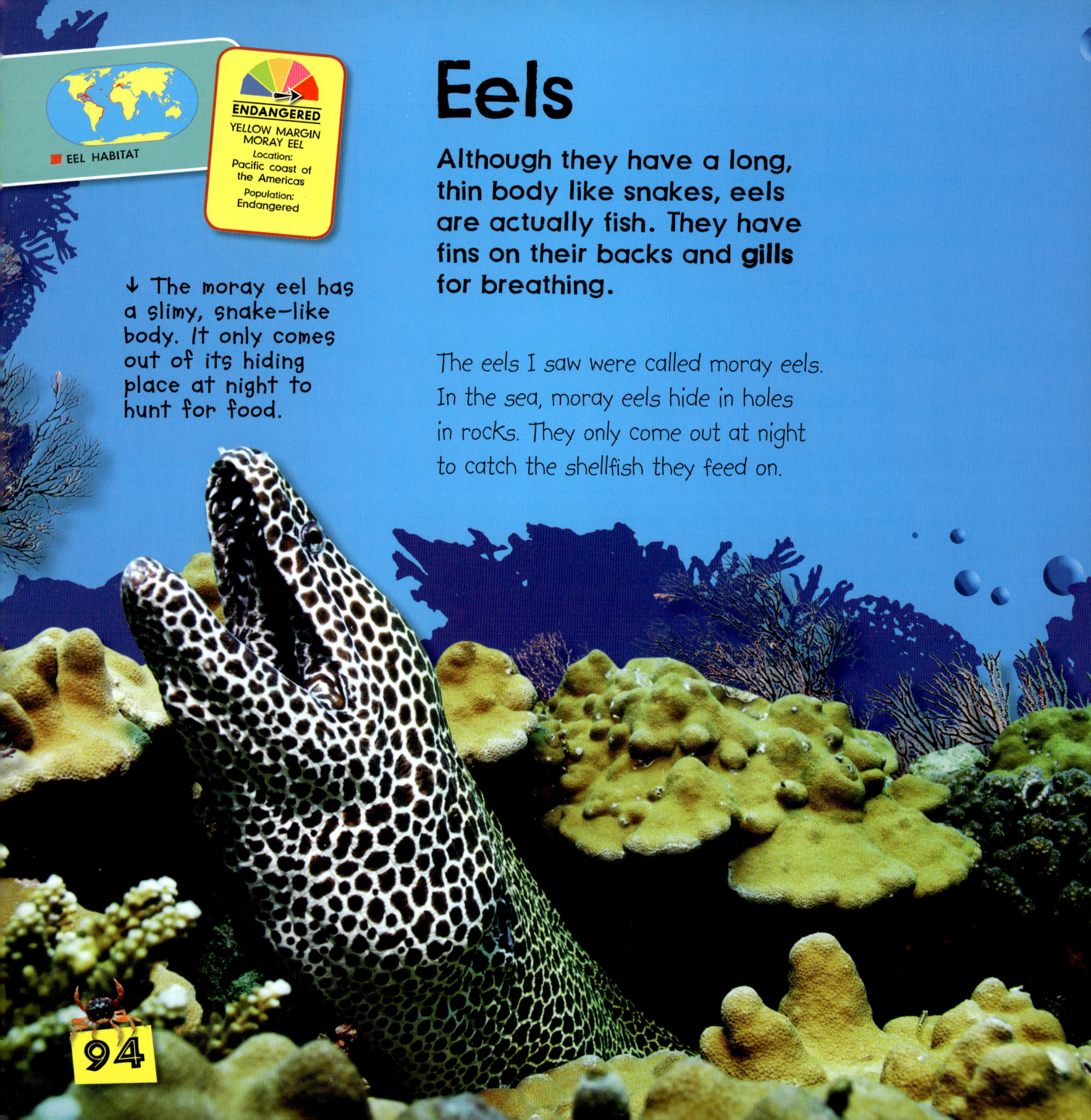

EEL HABITAT

ENDANGERED
YELLOW MARGIN MORAY EEL
Location: Pacific coast of the Americas
Population: Endangered

↓ The moray eel has a slimy, snake-like body. It only comes out of its hiding place at night to hunt for food.

Eels

Although they have a long, thin body like snakes, eels are actually fish. They have fins on their backs and **gills** for breathing.

The eels I saw were called moray eels. In the sea, moray eels hide in holes in rocks. They only come out at night to catch the shellfish they feed on.

The eels that live in lakes and rivers swim thousands of miles to the ocean, where they lay their eggs. About 3 years later, the young eels wriggle back into the rivers again. In some rivers in South America, the electric eel catches fish to eat by knocking them out with an electric shock.

↑ Freshwater eels swim huge distances from lakes and rivers far out into the Atlantic Ocean to lay their eggs.

Three things you didn't know about... EELS

1 There are about 600 kinds of eel living in fresh and salt water all over the world.

2 Young eels are called elvers.

3 The electricity produced by an electric eel is enough to shock a human being badly.

↑ The electric eel is actually a type of knife fish, not an eel, although it looks and swims like one.

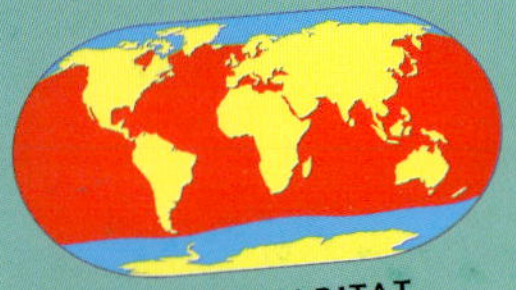

■ LOBSTER HABITAT

ENDANGERED
MOSAIC REEF CRAB
Location: Waters around Singapore
Population: Endangered — very rare

Crabs and Lobsters

Crabs and lobsters are not fish, even though they live in water. They are crustacean, so their body is covered with a hard shell that protects them from enemies.

As they grow, crabs and lobsters become too big for their shell. They have to shed the old shell so that a new, larger shell can grow.

↑ The boxer crab holds a sea anemone in each claw and waves their stinging tentacles at its enemies. The anemones eat the pieces of food the crab drops.

ZOO VIEW

Scientists in Australia are fixing concrete flowerpots to sea walls. The pots are new homes for crabs and other sea animals whose rock pool homes were destroyed when the walls were built.

→ Measuring up to 3 feet (1 meter) in length, the lobster uses its huge claws to crack open shellfish and feed on them at night.

Hermit crabs do not have their own shell. Instead, they live in the empty shell of another animal. The hermit crab I saw was living in the shell of a large **whelk**.

→ Hermit crabs mostly live on the seabed in warmer waters.

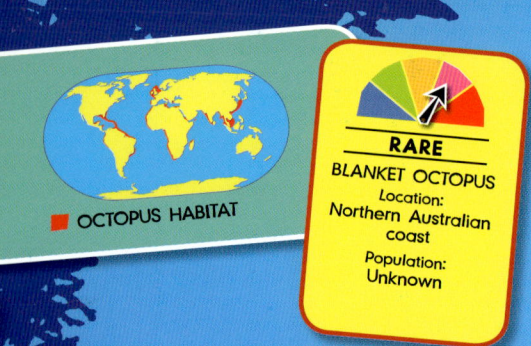

OCTOPUS HABITAT

RARE
BLANKET OCTOPUS
Location:
Northern Australian coast
Population:
Unknown

Octopuses and Squid

The octopus is a sea animal with eight long arms, called **tentacles**. These tentacles have suckers on them that can grip prey tight. A squid is similar to an octopus, but it has ten arms.

Sometimes octopuses walk along the seabed. They can also push themselves forward with a jet of water that they shoot out of their body. If an octopus thinks it is in danger, it squirts thick black ink into the water. This hides the octopus while it escapes.

→ The suckers on an octopus's tentacles help the animal to grip its prey and to fasten itself onto rocks.

body
suckers
eye
tentacle

Squid vary in size from about 1/2 inch (1.5 centimeters) long up to 65 feet (20 meters) long. Like octopuses, squid swim through the sea by shooting jets of water from their body.

ZOO STARS

In 2004, scientists found a glow-in-the dark giant squid in the Pacific Ocean near Japan. The scientists discovered that the squid uses its bright lights to dazzle and catch its prey.

↑ The squid can swim slowly by waving the flap-like fins along the sides of its body.

CORAL HABITAT

ENDANGERED
BLACK CORAL
Location: Mediterranean
Population: Endangered — very rare

Corals

Although **corals** look like flowers, they are huge groups of tiny sea animals with shells. Corals are mostly found in warm, clear sea water where there is lots of light.

↓ A coral reef teems with beautiful and unusual animals.

The corals I saw in the aquarium were pink, orange, and purple, but they come in other colors as well. Each tiny coral animal has stinging tentacles that stick out from its body. It uses these tentacles to catch tiny animals to eat.

→ Although they are animals, a lot of corals growing together look like an underwater garden.

← A coral reef like this takes thousands of years to grow.

Three things
that will help...
CORALS

1 Sometimes stores near the shore sell pieces of coral as souvenirs. Don't buy these, because when coral is collected, it kills the animals inside.

2 Don't walk on a coral reef. Coral animals are easily damaged.

3 Don't spill suncream in the ocean, because it might poison corals.

Thousands of years ago, corals formed rocky ridges called **reefs** on the seabed. Thousands of fish and other kinds of animals live in and around coral reefs. The reef shelters them and provides them with food.

DOLPHIN HABITAT

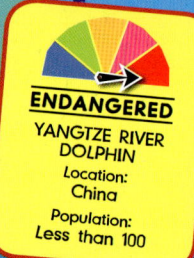
ENDANGERED
YANGTZE RIVER DOLPHIN
Location: China
Population: Less than 100

Dolphins

Dolphins are intelligent, graceful animals. Although they are shaped like a large fish, dolphins are really mammals like us.

Fish can stay underwater all their life, but dolphins have to keep coming up to the surface to breathe air.

teeth

← This dolphin has a large number of small, sharp teeth to help it catch and eat fish.

ZOO VIEW

Not all dolphins live in the ocean. Some types live in rivers. The World Wide Fund for Nature, or WWF, has been working in Cambodia to save the dolphins that live in the Mekong River. It is believed there are fewer than 100 of these dolphins left.

102

← River dolphins are dolphins that have swum up from the sea and have begun living in rivers.

In the ocean, dolphins live in groups. They swim near the surface, often jumping out of the water. They make clicking sounds and then listen for the **echoes** to bounce back from objects in the water. That is how they find their way and find the fish they eat.

↑ Dolphins often leap out of the water when they are playing.

↑ Dolphins feed their babies with milk from their body.

Spotter's Guide

CLOWNFISH

LENGTH **5.5 in (14 cm)**
WEIGHT **A few ounces (grams)**
HABITAT **West Pacific**

WHALE SHARK

LENGTH **45.9 ft (14 m)**
WEIGHT **Over 12.2 tons (12 tonnes)**
HABITAT **Tropical temperatures worldwide**

SMOOTH HOUND SHARK

LENGTH **5.2 ft (1.6 m)**
WEIGHT **26.5 lb (12 kg) or more**
HABITAT **East Atlantic and Mediterranean**

HAMMERHEAD SHARK

LENGTH **13.1–19.7 ft (4–6 m)**
WEIGHT **880 lb (400 kg)**
HABITAT **Tropical, sub-tropical, and temperate seas worldwide**

Quiz

How many arms does an octopus have?

Answer: Eight.

BASKING SHARK

LENGTH **26.2–32.8 ft (8–10 m)**
WEIGHT **6 tons (6 tonnes) or more**
HABITAT **Tropical and temperate seas worldwide**

FLOUNDER

LENGTH **4.7–17.7 in (12–45 cm)**
WEIGHT **26.9 lb (12 kg)**
HABITAT **North Atlantic**

OCTOPUS

LENGTH **11.8–35.4 in (30–90 cm)**
WEIGHT **6.6–22 lb (3–10 kg)**
HABITAT **Worldwide**

MANTA RAY

LENGTH **13.1–23 ft (4–7 m)**
WEIGHT **Over 1.8 tons (1.8 tonnes)**
HABITAT **Cool to warm seas worldwide**

PIRANHA

LENGTH **5.5–10 in (14–26 cm)**
WEIGHT **2.2 lb (1 kg)**
HABITAT **South American rivers and lakes**

SALMON

LENGTH **Up to 4.9 ft (1.5 m)**
WEIGHT **Up to 99.2 lb (45 kg)**
HABITAT **North Atlantic**

SQUID

LENGTH **0.7–45.9 ft ((0.2–14 m)**
WEIGHT **0.7–1000 lb (0.3 – 500 kg)**
HABITAT **Cool and temperate waters**

STINGRAY

LENGTH **19.7–23.6 in (50–60 cm)**
WEIGHT **4.4–8.8 lb (2–4 kg)**
HABITAT **East North Pacific**

Quiz

How does the fierce piranha hunt?

Answer: In large groups.

ELECTRIC EEL

LENGTH **Up to 8.3 ft (2.5 m)**
WEIGHT **Up to 44 lb (20 kg)**
HABITAT **Northern South America**

CONGER EEL

LENGTH **Up to 8.9 ft (2.7 m)**
WEIGHT **143 lb (65 kg)**
HABITAT **East North Atlantic, Europe, and Mediterranean**

MORAY EEL

LENGTH **Up to 61 in (157 cm)**
WEIGHT **Up to 154 lb (70 kg)**
HABITAT **Tropical seas**

EUROPEAN EEL

LENGTH **Up to 3.3 ft (1 m)**
WEIGHT **33 lb (15 kg)**
HABITAT **East North Atlantic, Mediterranean, Europe**

SEA HORSE

LENGTH **Up to 11.8 in (30 cm)**
WEIGHT **Variable**
HABITAT **Worldwide**

CORAL

LENGTH **Colony: 0.3–59 in (0.7–150 cm)**
WEIGHT **Variable**
HABITAT **Worldwide**

STARFISH

LENGTH **0.8 in–3.3 ft (2 cm–1 m)**
WEIGHT **Variable**
HABITAT **Worldwide**

BOXER CRAB

LENGTH **Up to 2 in (5 cm)**
WEIGHT **Up to 0.4 oz (10 g)**
HABITAT **Tropical saltwater**

Quiz

What happens when a starfish loses an arm?

Answer: It grows it right back!

RANCID CRAB

LENGTH **Up to 11.8 in (30 cm)**
WEIGHT **10.6–21 oz (300–600 g)**
HABITAT **European, Atlantic, African coast**

LOBSTER

LENGTH **Up to 3.3 ft (1 m)**
WEIGHT **Up to 44 lb (20 kg)**
HABITAT **Worldwide**

HERMIT CRAB

LENGTH **Around 0.8 in (2 cm)**
WEIGHT **Only a few ounces (grams)**
HABITAT **Sandy or muddy waters**

SEA ANEMONE

LENGTH **0.04 in – 32.8 ft (1 mm – 10 m)**
WEIGHT **Variable**
HABITAT **Worldwide**

My Day at the Zoo

Which of these animals did you see during your day at the zoo?
Try to describe what they were doing!

Lion
African elephant
Tiger
Jaguar
Giraffe
Zebra
Camel
Gray kangaroo
Parma wallaby
Vervet monkey
Pygmy marmoset
Chimpanzee
Orangutan
Panda
Koala
Crocodile
Python

- Alligator
- Chameleon
- Green turtle
- Blue and yellow macaw
- Toucan
- Ostrich
- Flamingo
- American bald eagle
- Golden eagle
- Great horned owl
- Sulphur-crested cockatoo
- Puffin
- Emperor penguin
- Clownfish
- Octopus
- Piranha
- Starfish

Which other animals did you see?

Glossary

Aviary A place to keep birds in.

Balance To keep steady.

Beak The hard part of a bird's mouth.

Breed To produce babies.

Camouflage Colors or shapes that make an animal match its surroundings.

Cold-blooded Having a body temperature that is the same as that of the surrounding air or water.

Coral A hard substance built up from the seabed by tiny animals.

Desert Very dry land where few plants can grow.

Echo A sound that bounces back and is heard again.

Enclosure An area with a fence or wall around it.

Endangered Describes an animal or plant that is in danger of becoming extinct.

Environment The surroundings of an animal or another living thing.

Extinct Not existing anymore; when every one of a kind of animal or plant has died out.

Fang A long, sharp tooth.

Gill One of the parts of a water animal's body that it uses to breathe underwater.

Grooming To clean hair or fur.

Herd A number of zebras, cows, or other animals living together.

Jaws The lower part of the face.

Mammal An animal that feeds on its mother's milk when it is young.

Mane The long hair on the back and neck of a lion, horse, or other animal.

Migrate To go to another country, or another part of the country, where more food can be found.

National park A large area of land where animals and plants are protected.

Nostril One of the two openings in the nose.

Poisonous Something that contains poison, which is a substance that can cause death or illness.

Pouch A bag for carrying things.

Predator An animal that catches and eats other animals.

Prey An animal that is hunted by other animals for food.

Ranger Someone who looks after a park or forest.

Reef A line of rock or coral just below or just above the surface of the sea.

Species A group of animals or plants that can breed together.

Talon One of the large claws on the foot of an eagle, owl, or some other bird of prey.

Tentacle A long feeler, like a bendable arm.

Tusk One of the two very long pointed teeth of an elephant. Other animals, such as walruses, boars, and narwhals, also have tusks.

Wading Walking through water.

Whelk A type of sea snail.

Wingspan The distance from one end of a bird's wing to the end of its other wing.

Index

Adelie penguin 76
African elephants 18–16
African lovebird 67
alligators 42–43
American bald eagle 62
American white pelican 73
Arabian camels 20–21
aviary 60, 61

babies 8, 10, 17, 19, 22, 25, 41, 42, 43, 51
Bactrian camels 20
beak 60, 61, 70, 72
big cat family 10
birds of prey 62
black coral 100

blanket octopus 98
boa constrictor 37
boxer crab 96
breeding 35, 43
Brookesia chameleon 47
brown pelican 73

California condor 8
calves 19
camels 20–21
camouflage 12, 46
capuchin monkeys 25
cats 10–11
chameleons 46–47
Chinese alligator 42, 43
clown fish 87
coats 12, 14, 16
cobras 36–37

cockatoo 67
cold-blooded animals 34
common boa 37
coral 100–101
crabs 96–97
crocodiles 34, 40–41
cubs 10

Dalmatian pelican 72
desert tortoise 49
dolphins 102–103

eagles 62–63
eels 94–95
eggs 34, 41, 43, 47, 49, 50, 51, 60, 74, 75, 77, 93
electric eel 95
elephants 18, 19
emperor penguin 77
extinction 9, 13
eyelashes 21

feathers 60, 61, 62, 68, 69
fins 87, 91, 93, 94, 99
fish 87, 88, 90, 92, 94
flamingos 70–71

flat fish 90–91
frilled lizard 44
fur and hair 8

Galapagos tortoise 48
geckos 37, 44
giant squid 99
Gila monster 45
gills 87, 94
giraffes 14–15
golden eagle 63
gray kangaroo 22
green peafowl 68
green-winged macaw 66
grooming 13

hammerhead shark 89
herds 16–19
hermit crab 97
Humboldt penguin 76

Indian starred tortoise 49

Jackson's chameleon 47
joeys 23

kangaroos 22–23
Klein's sole 90
knife fish 95

lionesses 10
lions 10–11
lizards 44–45, 46
lobsters 96–97
loggerhead turtle 50
lovebirds 67

mammals 8–31
manta ray 91
megamouth shark 88
milk 8
monkeys 24–25
moray eel 94
mosaic reef crab 96

Nile crocodiles 40

octopuses 98–99
ostriches 74–75

painted stork 70
panther chameleon 46
parrots 66–67
peacocks 68–69
pelicans 72–73
penguins 76–77
plaice 90–91

poison 36, 38, 45
pouch 22, 93
pride of lions 10
pygmy marmoset 25

rattlesnakes 38–39
rays 90, 91
red kangaroo 23
reefs 100–101
reptiles 34–57
river dolphins 102–103
royal python 37

saltwater crocodile 41
scales 34, 45
sea anemone 96
seabirds 72
sea horses 92–93
sea lion 88
serpent eagle 62
sharks 88–89

shell 48, 49, 50, 51, 96, 97, 100
shellfish 97
skin 34, 39, 45, 46,
smooth-hound shark 89
snakes 36–39
spider monkey 24
squid 98–99
storks 71
sulphur-crested cockatoo 67

tail 38, 39, 44, 47, 61, 68, 69, 76
talons 62
teeth 40, 41, 88, 102
terrapins 50–51
tigers 12, 13
tongue 14, 15, 45, 47,
tortoises 48–49

118

toucans 61
turtles 50–51

vervet monkeys 24–25
vultures 64–65

wading birds 70, 71
western diamondback rattlesnake 38
whale shark 89
white stork 71
white-tailed sea eagle 63
wings 60, 61, 65, 74, 76

Yangtze river dolphin 102
yellow-eared parrot 66
yellow margin moray eel 94

zebras 16–17

Notes for Parents and Teachers

- Discuss with the children why it is necessary to be quiet and not run when visiting a safari park, a reptile park, a bird park, or an aquarium. Why should you not tap on the glass in the tanks and why, in some areas, are you not allowed to use a camera with flash?

- Look through the book together. How many of the animals in the book can the children recognize?

- Some of the animals described in this book are fish, which are cold-blooded animals that have an internal skeleton and a backbone. Crabs, lobsters, octopuses, and squid do not have an internal skeleton. Crabs and lobsters have an external shell, while octopuses and squid have no skeleton at all, but have a body that is supported by the water. Dolphins are warm-blooded mammals.

- Discuss with your child what is meant by extinction and why some animals are in danger of becoming extinct. The main causes of extinction are hunting, the effects of pollution, and the destruction of the animals' natural habitats. If animal parks and zoos are able to breed endangered animals, they will not be able to release these animals into the wild unless a safe place can be found for them.

- Do the children have a favorite kind of animal? Why is this animal their particular favorite?

- Introduce the children to the word "camouflage." Look at the book together. Which of the animals are camouflaged? Can your child think of other animals which are camouflaged? Think particularly of animals that live in snowy areas.

- Some useful websites* for more information:
  www.bbc.co.uk/nature/animals/mammals
  www.thebigzoo.com
  www.nefsc.noaa.gov/faq
  www.kids.yahoo.com/animals
  www.allaboutbirds.org
  www.zsl.org/education/
  www.nwf.org/wildlife
  www.arkive.org
  www.uksafari.com
  www.mcsuk.org
  www.panda.org

* Website information is correct at time of going to press. However, the publishers cannot accept liability for any information or links found on third-party websites.